Economies of Whiteness

On the Social Ecology of White Liberals

MARC LOMBARDO

Ǝxousía PRESS

Share this book: with anyone, in any way, in whole or in part.

ISBN: 061580375X
ISBN-13: 978-0615803753

FOR CHELSEA MANNING

whose courage is a gift to the world

First, I must confess that over the past few years I have been gravely disappointed with the white moderate. I have almost reached the regrettable conclusion that the Negro's great stumbling block in his stride toward freedom is not the White Citizen's Counciler or the Ku Klux Klanner, but the white moderate, who is more devoted to "order" than to justice; who prefers a negative peace which is the absence of tension to a positive peace which is the presence of justice; who constantly says: "I agree with you in the goal you seek, but I cannot agree with your methods of direct action"; who paternalistically believes he can set the timetable for another man's freedom; who lives by a mythical concept of time and who constantly advises the Negro to wait for a "more convenient season." Shallow understanding from people of good will is more frustrating than absolute misunderstanding from people of ill will. Lukewarm acceptance is much more bewildering than outright rejection.

Martin Luther King, Jr.
"Letter from Birmingham Jail"

CONTENTS

CHAPTER ONE
What White Liberals Think of when They Think of Themselves: *Stuff White People Like* and White Liberal Identity

CHAPTER TWO
A Social Ecological Account of the White Liberal

ACKNOWLEDGMENTS

Praise and thanks to all those who inspired and nurtured this work materially, spiritually, and intellectually. In the words of Thelonious Monk, I mean *you*.

Foreword

The main intellectual thrust of this book consists of an attempt to render visible the material and spiritual contradictions that define white liberals in the present day United States. First and foremost, let me say that I do *not* regard white liberalism primarily as a political ideology but rather as a form of life.

This being said, do not let the naming of white liberals as the object of inquiry fool you: this is not primarily a book about identity. If this book were not so modest, perhaps it would endeavor to be a critique of identity as an imagined category that supposedly exists in isolation from global historical, political, and economic forces. In comparison with the standard of such a grand critical project, the work before you comes up rather short. On the basis of the modest task at hand, the only larger point I find myself able to make regarding identity is this: A social identity that fails to account for the conditions of labor upon which its existence depends is shaped by that lack of material understanding just as Oedipus' fate is sealed by his unawareness of the circumstances of his birth.

So much of the cultural work of whiteness consists in the erasure of the specific economic and social histories that narrate the production of modern racial categories as an embodiment of power relations. Whiteness is made and made over by the mutual workings and deployments of imperialism, colonialism, capitalism, migration, technology, science, medicine... we could go on. For that very reason, whiteness needs to be broken up and broken down along cultural, political, and economic lines before it can become a useful point of social inquiry.

Nearly 50 years after the Civil Rights Act, white supremacy still constitutes a significant lived reality for people of color and whites alike. The character of this lived reality has undoubtedly shifted in any number of significant ways. The myth of progress narrated every year during Black History Month would have us believe that these shifts in our lived experience align with the long arc of history as it bends toward justice. Upon examining the evidence, some of us are not entirely convinced that this is the case.

In the course of the investigation that follows, I seek to explicate the role played by white liberals in maintaining a political economy in which racial injustice comprises an essential dimension of the exploitation of the poor by the rich. I fail to see any means of accurately describing the social and economic violence endemic to the operation of many of our most central social institutions—educational, legal, economic, and ideological—without accounting for the role of white liberals in maintaining these institutions.

What would the media be without white liberals? What would our schools be without white liberals? What would the courts be without white liberals (e.g., public defenders)? What would labor unions be without the white liberals who comprise their managerial class? For that matter, what would our government be without the participation of white liberals (not only with respect to the white liberal politicians who comprise the ideological base of the Democratic Party but, perhaps just as significantly, in the deeply interrelated and aligned ideological apparatus that is the non-profit industrial complex)?

The difficulty encountered in the course of attempting the thought experiment proposed by these questions shows the extent to which many of the institutions most essential to the functioning of present US society would be very, very different than they are without the presence of white liberals. We have a bipartisan political consensus to thank for such absurdly brutal facts of 21st Century life as *The New Jim Crow* and the preservation of the carried-interest tax exemption (for who would want hedge fund managers paying taxes at rates comparable to us serfs?). While there may be a black man in the White House, the sociological data concerning differentials in income, wealth, employment, education, and incarceration are in my view as skewed against black folk today as they have been at any time since before The Great Society. If we are serious about redressing the racially focused violence inherent to the functioning of our economy and our society as a whole, then we need to become much, much more attentive to the role of white liberals in managing the institutions that enable and maintain such an antidemocratic and morally abject political consensus.

Too often, in the face of the continual efforts of the right to rescind voting rights, roll back educational desegregation, and ensure the perpetuation of a racial caste system by less overt means (e.g., by using the Drug War as the engine for the mass incarceration of black men in particular and poor people in general[1]) liberal institutions and individuals are given a pass. Yes, they could do more. Yes, they could do *some*thing. But they're all that's standing in the way of the Republicans! What choice do we have?!

In the face of this argument—if one can really call it an argument rather than a defense mechanism—I want to suggest a counter-intuitive hypothesis concerning the political function of liberalism in general and the social function of white liberals in particular. *What if* the fact that white liberals benefit from white supremacy is not simply an accident? *What if* the simplest explanation for the fact that white liberals are as ineffective as they are at preventing the economic and social violence that pervades our society is actually the best explanation? *What if* the truth about white liberals is that they are just as essential to the maintenance of white supremacy as those who administer state-sanctioned racially focused violence directly in their roles as cops, prison guards, prosecutors, judges, and civic leaders? *What if* it is actually the intellectual, spiritual, and moral bankruptcy of white liberals that constitutes the

---

[1] If anyone in any way doubts the systematic nature of the penal mechanisms deployed to ensure the preservation of the American caste system into the present day, Michelle Alexander's *The New Jim Crow* is a formidable resource.

greatest obstacle to redressing the most enduring and fundamental injustices in our society?

In confronting white liberals for their complacency and cowardice I offer this central principle: If you are certain that a solution exists that is in the best interest of all parties concerned, don't compromise! Ever! Few things are more detrimental to our political and intellectual culture than the fact that those few actors who even claim to be acting in the public interest do so from the supposedly reasoned and reasonable posture of being willing to compromise. Long hailed as a hallmark of bourgeois liberal political process, compromise presupposes that politics is a zero-sum game and it is this very conception of politics that is inherently compromised.

For this zero-sum notion of politics, deeply embedded within all sorts of influential political philosophies from *Realpolitik* to identity politics: a gain for one constituency or interest (e.g., the environment) is necessarily a loss for another (e.g., the economy); values such as freedom, security, justice, and equality are presupposed to be in conflict with one another; and, finally the best that can be hoped for from any given policy is an appropriate balancing of these supposedly mutually-incompatible values. Far from being the enemy of zero-sum politics, the making of mutually-unsatisfactory compromises is its definitive hallmark.

If I truly believe that my solution is not only better for me but better for you as well, my willingness to abandon that solution in favor of a mutually-unsatisfactory compromise is an insult to both of us. A mutually-unsatisfactory compromise is the mark of a failure of persuasion, imagination, perspiration, integrity, humility, and common decency. Such failures do indeed happen, but why on Earth we should prize them as an ideal basis for political consensus I cannot imagine.

In conclusion, I offer these words of advice and encouragement to all those interested in destabilizing the ideological hegemony of white liberals: Give no passes and give no fucks! Call bullshit at any and every opportunity! If telling the truth means blowing up your career, then blow up your career! I mean torpedo that shit! Go on food stamps if you have to! I mean that! The essential question for white liberals to confront is this: Would you rather be a moderately compensated slave or poor and free?

An Overview

The first full-length chapter of the present book consists of a study of the now moribund popular humor website *Stuff White People Like* (SWPL). This may seem like a curious choice for careful study given that I am likely only recapitulating a cultural phenomenon that would otherwise be all but dead. Even when I started writing the present work in 2010, I was already aware that I was somewhat late to the party as far as SWPL's cultural relevance was concerned. It was clear to me at the time that a series of rather strict limits concerning what SWPL would and would not make fun of were essential to making SWPL's brand of humor as popular as it certainly was for a short period of time. Given the strictness of these limits, it is of little surprise to me that the endeavor ran out of steam long ago. Nevertheless, I am confident that the effort to examine such an ephemeral cultural artifact not only has much of significance to say to us today but that it may very well help shape our understanding of the future of cultural politics as well. Even Adorno found it worth his time to tarry with astrology columns, thereby making the columns in question of significance long after what otherwise would have been their expiration date.

As I show, SWPL was never really concerned with white people as a whole, but exclusively with the subset that is white liberals. In fact, the website strives unerringly to provide the appearance that whites who are not liberal (e.g., rednecks and the elite) do not exist. Such an omission leads to a fundamental misunderstanding of the nature of white privilege, even as it pertains to the white liberals who are supposedly being lampooned by the website. On the other hand, SWPL is often quite dead-on with respect to its description of the contradictions of white liberal culture when considered unto itself. As such, by interrogating the deeper socioeconomic significance of the cultural phenomena that SWPL describes, the characterization of white liberals featured by the website provides an excellent jumping off point for understanding white liberals as a function of their environment.

The next chapter of the book attempts to build upon the characterization of white liberal identity attained from SWPL by providing a naturalistic account of the white liberal as a biological species unto itself. This analysis proceeds by providing a more explicit account of the social, economic, and cultural contradictions that define the circumstances of white liberal existence. Economically, white liberals are exempted from the most exploitative forms of labor, but unlike the rich, they do not profit directly from the exploitation of the working class other than in their capacity as consumers. Socially, white liberals primarily live in isolated enclaves such as newly gentrified urban neighborhoods and suburban college towns which scarcely allow them opportunities to engage with other social groups (e.g., the working class) except in the context of service economies. Culturally, white liberals often find themselves occupying a passive, consumption-driven relationship to cultural artifacts, as opposed to the often dynamic and participatory culture of the working class; moreover, unlike the rich, white liberals lack the economic means to shape the aesthetic values of consumer culture. Cumulatively, these contradictions define the position white liberals occupy with respect to the architectonic organization of human socioeconomic activity at present, i.e., capitalism.

Today, as members of postindustrial societies, it is often only through capitalist white supremacist institutions that we eat, live, and breath—although these fundamental activities are denied to more and more of us every day, often on the basis of the dictates of capitalism and white supremacy. If we want the world to work differently, and for all of our sake we certainly should want this, first we have to confront the way that it actually works today—i.e., the way that actually existing institutions serve people's needs to whatever extent that they do. For this reason, this work is primarily one of analysis rather than prescription. If there is an occasion for a guarded optimism, it lies in the possibility that we find and build institutions from within the present social and economic conditions that serve to encourage the ongoing revision and alteration of those most pervasive and pernicious features of contemporary society: capitalism and white supremacy.

I do indeed believe that artistic, cultural, and intellectual works can play a significant role in transforming economic, political, and social circumstances. (If I didn't, I would not bother to produce such works.) However, I also believe that the transformative potential of cultural works depends upon their understanding the limitations of existing institutions and attempting to surpass them. Use whatever institutions you can so long as you don't have to compromise who or what you are. If there's no institution that lets you do that, build your own! It may be small, but at least no one can tell you what (not) to say.

A Note on Method

0.1   *From Cultural Politics to Social Ecology by way of Political Economy*

While this book constructs its analysis in large part by engaging with expressions of white liberal cultural identity, this is above all in the interest of critically de-reifying that cultural identity with respect to its historico-material forces. If this work makes any contribution whatsoever to the broader task of social theory it is a rather modest one that can be summarized as follows: the harder a given identity works to conceal its material conditions, the more determining those conditions are for the identity in question.

The underlying presumption of this observation is essentially this: you don't really know a culture until you know the relationships through which it pays for itself. While this formulation does indeed highlight the immediacy of economic relationships with respect to the formation of cultural identity, in no way is this immediacy determinative in the last instance. Economic relations are themselves always already conditional upon and conditioned by a host of distinct endogenously and exogenously valued relations (e.g., to culture, to history, to technology, and, especially, to nature).

The central question of inquiry for the present work is essentially the following: what role do white liberals play in the *political economy* of whiteness?

11

The term "white liberal" suggests that the group in question is defined chiefly by racial identity and political ideology. The point I wish to make is a relatively, perhaps deceptively, simple one: How white liberals make their living has everything to do with their cultural and political identification. From this view, "white liberal" implies not simply a cultural identity but also a particular socio-economic role that exists in relation to the economy as a whole.

Methodologically speaking, my position is this: until and unless we view cultural identity as deeply conjoined with economic reality at every level of analysis, we deprive ourselves of a more robust understanding of both how culture forms the iterations it does and how (and for whom) the economy works. I call this view deceptively simple not only because I found it incredibly challenging to employ such a thoroughly dialectical method in the course of producing the thoughts collected herein (what at first seemed like a project that would require only a few hours ended up taking a number of years). It also seems to me, in hindsight, that many others who would likely accept this dialectical view concerning the relationship between culture and economics as a theoretical statement often reach a point in their analyses where they fail to put this dialectic into practice.

For his failure to recognize the fact that is right in front of his face—that white supremacy is in and of itself an economic value—Thomas Frank is something like the *bête noire* of this book, god bless him. Joan

Walsh attempts to make the racial problematic implicit in Frank's work explicit in her book title *What's the Matter with White People?* Walsh suggests that it is not necessarily their attachment to values issues (e.g., prayer in schools, abortion, etc.) so much as it is their adherence to the identity of whiteness that compels uneducated whites to vote Republican. I accept this point as far as it goes, but it is my view that we don't really understand white supremacy at all until we understand it 1) as a defining condition of existing economic relations and 2) as a systematic feature of present society that spans the political and ideological spectrum.

Indeed, the significance of race as a factor in a person's life chances is altogether too prominent and too consistent across the country's regions for the institutional mechanisms that insure these outcomes to be merely localized and partial. For instance, many Northern and Western states have higher rates of African-American incarceration than states in the Deep South.[2] We cannot even recognize, much less understand, the near ubiquity of white supremacy as a force in American society that crosses regional and ideological barriers—as the statistics clearly demonstrate—until we take seriously the possibility

---

[2] To take a particularly dramatic example, African-American men in California were incarcerated at a rate of 5,525 per 100,000 in the year 2010 (i.e., a rate that is over eight times that of white men in one of the bluest of states and considerably higher than the already unconscionable national average incarceration rate for African-American men of 3,074 per 100,000). See: Joseph M. Hayes, "California's Changing Prison Population," http://www.ppic.org/main/publication_show.asp?i=702

that white liberals perform an integral role in the perpetuation of white supremacy.

If we are to follow the analysis of whiteness, economics, and ideology to its most logical conclusion, and if we are serious about ending white supremacy in the long term or ameliorating its most pernicious social outcomes in the short-term, we simply have no choice but to deeply examine the role of white liberals. While white liberals are to a certain extent willing to acknowledge the readily demonstrable fact that they benefit from white privilege, our analysis must go deeper. We must demonstrate the fact that white liberals simply could not exist in the manner that they do without the function that they perform in maintaining white supremacy. A fundamental relationship to white supremacy defines white liberals both in terms of their immediate economic interests (short-sighted as these are) and their fundamental self-awareness (both as it is lacking in certain critical respects and entirely excessive in other relatively trivial ones).

Understanding the relationship between the cultural values of white liberals and the particular social, economic, and ideological constraints that define their existence will in turn improve our understanding of how white supremacy functions in the 21st Century. Such an analysis also affords the opportunity—only insofar as it remains fiercely contentious of white liberals' justifications, excuses, and defense mechanisms concerning their role in white supremacy—for understanding how white liberals themselves are duped by their political ideology. That is, I believe that Thomas Frank's description of white lower-income values voters as being victims of misplaced ideological loyalty—i.e., by voting for Republicans despite it being supposedly to their own economic detriment—is no less (and perhaps somewhat more) true of white liberals' unerring loyalty to Democrats. To state only the most blatantly obvious of examples: It was Bill Clinton who brought us financial securities deregulation and media consolidation and it is Barack Obama who is trying so vigorously to reduce social security benefits.

White supremacy and capitalism go together like peas and carrots. The central task before us is to elucidate the manner in which white liberal culture—if it may be so-called—performs an economically valued function with respect to the maintenance of exploitative social relations. Essentially, the political economic work white liberals perform amounts to this: they serve to obfuscate the fact that white supremacist violence is integral to the functioning of the economy as a whole as it is presently constituted. The white liberal cultural ideology of "equality of opportunity" provides an invaluable alibi for the ongoing systematic exploitation of the poor in general and those of darker complexion in particular.

The left hand and the right hand may work according to the most extraordinarily divergent means but we should not be so naïve as to assume that this is itself any indication that they are not in fact working in concert. The hand alone knows not why it does what it does nor toward what end. Even if the brain is nowhere to be found—and it usually isn't, particularly with respect to politics—we can still look at the cumulative nature of the work performed and ask how it functions and who it serves. With respect to such considerations, the question of intentions is secondary if it is relevant at all. I'm sick of white people's good intentions.

0.1.1   The Return to Political Economy

Let us not be too discouraged. Resources for fighting the collective delusion of short-term economic thinking, which constitutes the deracinated deethnicized decultured declassed depoliticized unconscious core of whiteness as an identity fetish, abound even in the most seemingly unlikely of places. Oddly enough, the white liberal tradition of political economy is one such place. While neoclassical economics ostensibly draws its intellectual lineage from this tradition, it also rejects what are in fact the most important and distinguishing characteristics and contributions of classical political economic thought as supposedly somehow less than scientifically precise (when, in fact, it is actually the non-falsifiable perversion that is the neoclassical view that has nothing to do with science in any meaningful sense of the word).

I take the main contributions of political economy to be the following: 1, every mode of production requires a qualitatively corresponding mode of consumption and vice versa (i.e., I take Say's Law to hold qualitatively—with respect to modes of production—rather than assuming a readily quantifiable equivalence between acts of production and consumption); 2, modes of production and consumption both require qualitatively corresponding social agents and vice versa (i.e., any given social agent is constituted by particular modes of production and consumption) and; 3, all acts of production and consumption consist in natural metabolic relationships that can never be definitively quantified or fully equated quantifiably but which in the last instance determine all subsequent quantifiable relations.

These doctrines of political economy effectively announce a series of limits concerning the study of economics upon which the scientific status of that study effectively depends. According to these doctrines, methodologically speaking, political economy as a body of thought is only itself there where it is stubbornly negative and critical of any so-called "economics" that: 1) privileges the calculation of quantitative formulae over the understanding of qualitative phenomena; 2) ignores the predisposition of particular social agents toward particular modes of production and consumption and/or; 3) ignores the role of economics itself as a particular mode of production and consumption performed by particular social agents with a particular relationship to natural metabolic processes. Both the first and the last object of political economic critique is the discipline of economic calculus itself as formulated at any given time and place (i.e., under particular political economic conditions) with respect to: the prejudices it holds, the observable facts it all-too-conveniently denies or dismisses, and the question of who benefits from its attendant blind spots and prejudices.

In an article entitled "The Lost Science of Classical Political Economy" that is worth quoting from at length, one of the greatest contemporary proprietors of political economy, Michael Hudson, discusses what he sarcastically calls "the riddle" of neoclassical economics:

> There is a seeming riddle in the recent evolution of economic thought. It has become more otherworldly and abstract, more detached from the reality of how economies are running deeper into debt to a financial oligarchy.[...] Yet academic orthodoxy treats this as anomalous, side-stepping the two key features of today's economic crisis: the "magic of compound interest" multiplying debts owed by the bottom 90 percent of the population to savers among the top 10 percent, while industrial capitalism is turned into a "tollbooth economy" by privatizing rent-extracting privileges on what used to be the public domain.
>
> Academic rationalizers of today's economic policy use models that deny that such a failure could exist in the first place. Yet

mathematically inclined economists claim that their discipline has become a science.[...] The mathematical boys confuse social sciences grounded in history and jockeying for political power with the universals of physics. [...]

Pseudo-science wielded on behalf of special interests turns mathematical abstraction into a vehicle to strip away what used to be the major concern of classical political economy, and indeed economic reform, over the past two centuries. The aim of classical value and price theory was to isolate land rent, monopoly rent, and financial interest and fees (and "capital" gains) as a free lunch accruing to privilege.

From this perspective, it is no wonder that neoclassical economists dismiss many of the most salient contributions of classical political economy at all costs. Ignoring the tradition of economic thought is essential to the modern economist's job description— i.e., providing ideological cover for the extractive business practices of the 1%. The better part of the tradition of economic thought simply must be dismissed because it offers means that are simply far too useful for the task of distinguishing between the value earned in production and the unearned value that accrues to those who do nothing more than exercise the privilege of absentee ownership.[3]

---

[3] At present, the privilege of usurious extortion allotted to the

In addition to the analysis of the collection of unearned rents, and the politics of class struggle that this analysis implies, there is another feature in many of the works of classical political economy that is almost equally disturbing to contemporary economists. Namely, the troubling insistence that, no matter how industrial its form may appear, human economic production always consists of a fundamental relationship to nature. For neoclassical economists, there is even something profoundly dangerous about the perspective of an author who, as Hudson notes, was the chief apologist for the bankers of his day, David Ricardo. In the following passage, the first two sentences of Ricardo's *Principles of Political Economy and Taxation*, note the essential continuity between economic phenomena and natural phenomena (my emphasis):

---

rich is insured through the publicly financed assistance of state violence—i.e., as in the case of law enforcement performing evictions at the behest of the financial sector, whose rights to the properties in question stem from fraud in more cases than not. In 2012, the Assessor of San Francisco, Phil Ting, found that in the sample of foreclosure records that his office reviewed from the preceding years, there was a "clear violation of law" in 84% of cases. While highly geographically limited in scope, this finding is nevertheless deeply suggestive of the widespread nature of fraudulent practices in the mortgage industry before, during, and after the sub-prime mortgage crisis. For further details, see Ting's press conference:
http://www.youtube.com/watch?v=hVyca1ecQRg

The produce of the earth—all that is derived from its surface by the united application of labour, machinery, and capital, is divided among three classes of the community; namely, the proprietor of the *land*, the owner of the stock or capital necessary for its *cultivation*, and the labourers by whose industry it is *cultivated*.

But in different stages of society, the proportions of the *whole produce of the earth* which will be allotted to each of these classes, under the names of rent, profit, and wages, will be essentially different; depending mainly on *the actual fertility of the soil*, on the accumulation of capital and population, and on the skill, ingenuity, and instruments employed in *agriculture*.

What would it mean for economics to take this emphasis upon the fundamentally ecological nature of economic production found in Ricardo and other classical political economists literally? Are we really so hubristic and oblivious as to think that through industrialism we have somehow overcome ecological reality for good as if it were a mere historical anachronism? Upon reflection, what basis do we have for making *any* analysis or inquiry that fails to recognize the inherent inseparability of economic and ecological phenomena?

While economic textbooks may cite the names of early white liberal authors such as Smith and Ricardo with reverence, the cumulative and systematic effect of such textbooks is to eradicate the most enduring and relevant contributions of these authors for the understanding of present realities. One might think that if white liberals are indeed genuinely compelled by the values (such as, e.g., environmentalism) that they often espouse, they would draw from the authority of these historical resources much more thoroughly and critically than they do.[4] But then white liberals understand too well that their whiteness depends upon keeping the realities of history at a certain length in favor of the present prejudices of a "science" that is unworthy of the name.

As far as whiteness is concerned, the very idea of history of all sorts (intellectual, genealogical, national, financial, spiritual, etc.) is a fundamentally troubling proposition. Upon reflection, no lineage is ever quite white enough for white people, including their own. History, even in its whiter moments, must be continually and perpetually whitewashed for the sake of the promise of the whiteness to come for all one day in the future. The promise of the free market—in which opportunity is infinitely elastic, barriers to entry (e.g., skin color, poverty) don't exist, and nature has been definitively transcended—depends upon denying both the past and the present for their failure to match up with the pure whiteness imaginable only in the by and by. Anyone who states the obvious fact that this imaginary promise serves only those who

---

[4] The work of Amartya Sen provides a few suggestions on this point.

need it the least is in turn blamed for setting back the promise's implementation; in fact, it is the promise itself that is empty and which, by its very definition, could never be implemented. What a remarkable project of abstraction undertaken at the behest of the few and in service to no one! Plato would be proud.

0.1.2   *Ledge Dwelling: On the Dilemma of Neoclassical Economics*

By calling for a return to political economy, I wish to invoke the Enlightenment tradition of white liberal thought at the direct expense of the mass of charlatans who claim to be practitioners of economic science today. In fact, neoclassical economists have as little understanding of the word "science" as they have of the word "economics." "Science" concerns the process of formulating one's ideas about the world in such a way as to identify a possible result that if encountered in experience would definitively show one's ideas to be wrong. "Economics" is the study of the processes and apparatus concerning the human organism's metabolic relationship to nature. Thus, neoclassical economics is neither science nor is it economics. Discuss.

The methods of neoclassical economics are the opposite of those methods that can legitimately be called scientific just as its aims are actually the opposite of any meaningful sense of economics. The standard of falsifiability is one that no neoclassical economist will ever submit to. This is readily apparent with respect to the fact that these "pond scum"—to use economist Dean Baker's term for his neoclassical colleagues—continue to recommend the cutting of public spending (i.e., austerity) as a means of solving fiscal crises despite invariable evidence that such measures only make fiscal crises worse. Such behavior seems quizzical at best. But then, the aim of neoclassical economics is not to economize. In fact, its aim is to move humanity further and further from the relationship to nature that we in fact are.

As natural beings on an unsupported flight of fancy, we had better save some energy and resources for the landing or else it won't be much of a landing at all. Quite possibly because they are for the most part a bunch of upper middle class white men (and the students and disciples of upper middle class white men who share a fundamentally white supremacist epistemology and temperament) economists refuse to accept this. We must fly higher and higher at all costs, they say. If your needs (like, say, oxygen) are not taken care of, blame those who say we must go back down closer to Earth and not those who hoarded all the oxygen tanks for themselves on the way up.

Neoclassical economics is among the last vestiges of the modern university that continue to conceive of knowledge on the Platonic model in which research consists primarily of thinking really really hard about what logically must be (i.e., what you most want to be) and only secondarily if at all in bothering to look around in order to find out what actually is. When 100 years ago, John Dewey claimed that we are not yet modern in our thinking, this is exactly the sort of thing that he meant. By this measure I'm afraid that, far from being postmodern, we are still nearly as far from reaching any modernity worthy of the name as we were in Dewey's day.

Unsurprisingly, the extent to which work challenging to the neoclassical model takes place in university economics departments, it does so almost exclusively within the data-driven subfield of econometrics. Unfortunately, it is an academic field's dominant theoretical model (rather than the nature of the data that it uncovers through observation) that primarily determines the resources allotted to, and the extra-disciplinary influence of, that field. While the practice of science compels inquirers to hold data above theory, the interpretation of available data is always disproportionately influenced by the theoretical models accepted and funded at any given time.

Reality is structured in such a way that it will invariably frustrate our imagined models—that is, if and when we take the trouble to look at it with any care. But then when has a Platonist ever been convinced by an argument from observation (and today's economists are nothing if not Plato's children)? There is nothing in the nature of reality to prevent—and, indeed, given its often intractable nature, there is in fact much to encourage—a devout Platonist from holding reality itself in contempt for failing to match up with his imagination! This logic, infallible on its own terms but nevertheless fundamentally schizophrenic, might be the punch line of a joke if it were not so definitively implicated in (if not chiefly responsible for) the foamingly vicious and drastically unnecessary inequality and ecological destruction that is the hallmark of the present world economic system.

While the lack of scientific understanding evident in the remnants of Platonism that comprise present "economics" is certainly a scourge of the Earth, it is also true that science evangelists—I'm looking at you my atheist friends—also need a healthy dose of humility. As a first corrective, they should recall that while a science's dominant theory determines where its money goes, the money that goes into a science also determines its theory. That is to say, the dominant theoretical model of a given discipline is often decided by whatever model attracts the most resources. You'd think this point would be obvious to economists but then they have a considerable interest in not recognizing the degree to which their model of "science" is conditional upon the material support (e.g., grants, fellowships, and endowments) of the rich, who it is their job to serve by producing conducive ideology.

While neoclassical economics doesn't do a very good job at describing the world, it does indeed work remarkably well for neoclassical economists. Provided they maintain their ideological purity, and don't ask too many questions concerning where money comes from, such economists have the option of making millions if not billions on Wall St. The crux of the problem is this: When given the choice between doing science for the love of knowledge or doing science for a fortune which would you choose? All other things being equal—as economists like to say, despite knowing full well that no two options ever are equal when considered in all of their various aspects—why not adopt a belief system that enriches you? There can be no doubt: in its function as an ideology factory for the rich, neoclassical economics makes at least 99% of us poorer.

Indeed, economists have quite the hustle going. However, if this is any consolation, and really it's not, they're completely miserable thanks largely to the success of the ideology that is the cause of their own success. This ideology requires that its adherents: deny the existence of the natural world in both its limits and non-quantifiable capacities, regard everyone else as having the thievish mentality exemplified by their own ideology, and feel an unbounded (fundamentally religious) sense of duty to sustain the current unjust and unsustainable flight of fancy. For this fundamentally childish worldview, nature is conceived of as nothing more than a tool for our tools, as if its parts can simply be replaced as soon as they start to wear out. Economists themselves benefit from their infinite hubris only in a merely monetary fashion (i.e., as opposed to the salubrious pleasure afforded by a genuinely economic life of modest means, the moderation of moderation, and awareness of and participation in an ever larger portion of the chain of relationships that constitute one's own consumption and production).

Even if the name of their delusion is Rationality—conceived as an end in itself, and defined in absurdly narrow terms—there is nothing whatsoever rational about it because it deliberately guards itself against considering alternatives. It is their single-minded devotion to the world of their own delusions, their distance from the consequences of their own actions, and their conscious alignment with the forces of greatest social violence that remove economists from feeling the immediate effects of the calculated economic fire that it is their job to set. Stand with us up here if you don't want to get burned, they say, coaxing us to join them on a ledge carefully designed so as to hold as few as possible.

Living on a ledge is not easy. It requires constant vigilance. Even the slightest movement carries the possibility of peril. It's best not to look down. And all the awhile, though his immediate comfort requires that he not dwell too long on this fact, in the back of his head, the economist knows that it is only a matter of time before the ledge will give way. He knows this because, after all, he helped set the building on fire in the first place.

Economists are by no means the only ones on this ledge. But just about everyone on this ledge thinks like an economist. The social cohesion of ledge dwellers is above all else ensured by adherence to a single taboo. What must not be said, at any cost, at any time, at any place, is the very fact that from the outside appears the most obvious and important thing to say: "The fucking building is on fire!"

For anyone with an outside perspective, putting out the fire that is in the process of consuming the entire building seems the only sensible course of action, even for the survival of the ledge dwellers themselves. Nevertheless, among ledge dwellers, such thinking is derided as hopeless, unrealistic, and dangerous. Even the most inquisitive and imaginative among the ledge dwellers stops at asking merely how to enlarge and/or better secure the ledge. No one on the ledge can even think of the possibility of putting out the fire because that would mean going back into the burning building and fighting alongside those poor souls the ledge dwellers abandoned in order to secure their space on the ledge in the first place. Indeed, going back into the building would mean confronting the flames at their source and the first who do so will almost certainly be putting themselves in a position of greater immediate discomfort if not danger.

In other words, the mentality of short-term economic thinking is itself a "public choice" problem. The first to abandon this mentality pay the greatest price for it. In theory, the way of solving such a problem is to propose a pact for collective action once consensus is reached. If ledge dwellers agree to fight the fire collectively, they can thereby ameliorate the risk faced by any single individual (and enhance the overall likelihood of success). Unfortunately, however, there is already a prior collective pact of sorts operating in practice on the ledge: anyone who proposes collective action to fight the fire loses their place on the ledge. In such circumstances, it is up to the minority of collectively interested parties who recognize the ledge's inherent precarity—even if this is only a minority of one—to take direct action in wresting whatever resources they need for fighting the fire from the other ledge dwellers.

No amount of ledge dwellers, no matter their number, ever makes a true majority until and unless that majority acts in the interest of preserving the building as a whole. Whatever their level of internal consensus, no matter how close to absolute such a position may be among the ranks of ledge dwellers, the agreement not to fight the fire is only tenable insofar as it is forged out of a collective delusion to ignore the material circumstances faced by those inside the building. By definition, ledge dwellers are always and only a minority compared to those who face the flames directly (with far fewer resources).

It is for similar reasons that Thoreau and James Baldwin argued that any minority more right than their neighbors and more decent to the dispossessed constitutes the only true majority. No matter their numbers, this majority of sense and integrity has not only the right but the moral *obligation* to act rather than to wait for their delusional counterparts to come to their senses and decency. Seeing only the logic of preserving their own immediate preoccupations, regardless of the costs of these preoccupations to anyone else and even to themselves in the end, the delusional are susceptible to neither arguments from data nor arguments from compassion. Economists, and anyone who takes seriously their patently absurd recommendations for the swift engineering of human suffering (i.e., austerity), belong in padded cells rather than university offices, think tanks, and corporate suites.

If I've chosen to dwell somewhat metaphorically on the case of economists, it's because this minority is particularly influential in maintaining the collective delusion of ledge dwelling that defines the exclusionary social strategy of both white supremacy and capitalism. Myopic, misguided, short-term economic thinking and white supremacy go hand-in-hand. In fact, narrowing public debate to the confines of the logic of short-term economics is essential for denying the social violence that our economic system engenders, particularly for people of darker complexion who are on the front lines.

Each day, it grows harder and harder to deny the obvious: the building is on fire. Those on the ledge have a choice: they can become firefighters with the rest of us or they can watch like Lady Macbeth as we all burn. Though such a consequence may not seem immediate until it is too late, when they fan the flames for their own short-term gains, ledge dwellers seal their fate along with everyone else's. Like it or not, all of us will be together one way or another: either in struggle or in death.

A Note on Terminology

0.2   Coarse-Grained   Analysis   Deserves   Coarse Terminology

The terminology employed in this book is rather coarse in nature. I apologize in advance if this choice of terminology offends your sensibilities and I hope that the book will have something to offer you despite this transgression. I chose to use such coarse terms in the effort to express the coarse-grained nature of the analysis offered herein. Our primary concern is not to understand white liberals as a cultural phenomenon unto themselves. Rather, we seek to understand the unique role white liberals play with respect to the unified function of whiteness (across the diversity of political and cultural affiliations) in the larger political economy of capitalist exploitation. In order to focus upon this bigger picture, and the largely unobserved role of white liberals in contributing to this picture, it was necessary to sacrifice a certain level of detail with respect to the depiction of the social groups under consideration.

For instance, I segment whites into three more or less distinct groups that are by no means comprehensive or even particularly descriptive with respect to the sociocultural identification of any particular member: rednecks (rural, exurban, or suburban uneducated Republicans of all but the highest wealth bracket), white liberals (urban or suburban educated Democrats of all but the highest wealth bracket), and elites (the wealthiest 5% or thereabouts of whites regardless of political identification). Obviously, there are many individuals who fit nowhere in such a coarsely portrayed landscape (e.g., educated and uneducated urban Republicans who are not wealthy, educated and uneducated rural Democrats, uneducated urban Democrats, etc.). Moreover, by no means are these categories intended to be comprehensive expressions of identity; any given individual is sure to be richer in complexity than the generalizations which I will make about these coarsely defined groups. Again, the intention was not to depict the entire range of individuals and experiences that comprise all of the various forms of whiteness. Rather, my goal was simply to provide an outline, in the broadest and most general strokes, of how certain culturally and socially distinct segments of whites (focusing upon those segments most influential with respect to the social, cultural, and economic maintenance of white supremacy) relate to one another.

0.2.1 Stop Calling it "Racism," Start Calling it "White Supremacy"

Let us proceed to discuss the next important term at work in the present investigation that would likely benefit from a bit of commentary and clarification: white supremacy. Generally speaking, white liberals prefer to use the term "racism" when discussing racial injustice rather than white supremacy. In fact, they almost never refer to white supremacy except with respect to persons and/or groups who explicitly self-identify as white supremacist (what a better example of identity politics!).

It would seem then that "racism" covers a much broader range of phenomena. Indeed, white supremacy is the explicit name for the motive of organizations, institutions, and individuals that utilize and facilitate violence for the express purpose of inflicting social, economic, and physical harm upon people of color. By contrast, the most common usage of racism generally connotes the race-based prejudices, biases, and stereotypes of individuals and groups. The difference is clear: racism is a matter of representations and perceptions, whereas white supremacy conveys an agent's interest in *enacting* the named condition. It is my view that there is at present on the whole altogether too much talk of racism and altogether too little talk of white supremacy. By referring primarily to perceptions rather than actions, "racism" has lost much of its meaning.

"We are all racist," is a saying that white liberals are known to solemnly intone as a confession of personal guilt for their internal monologues, which they nevertheless assure us they do their best not to act upon. The distinction between a person's internal monologues and his or her actions is an important one to take note of generally speaking; unfortunately, in this case, the function of asserting this distinction is largely to smuggle in the assumption that preventing racist actions is simply a matter of individuals not acting upon their racist monologues. Accordingly, the problem of racism is turned into an atomistic, individualized problem of intentions rather than a collective, social problem of outcomes. From there, it is not a very great leap to see that the adjective "racist" is applied almost exclusively as a description of offensive verbal slurs and characterizations. All but forgotten is the extent to which racial injustice is a matter of the historical and continuing institution of physical violence.

Anyone can claim to be offended on more or less any grounds. By contrast, the claim that one has experienced violence is an empirical claim. It requires a certain amount of evidence and a certain consistency in the standards used to evaluate evidence from one case to another. Accordingly, I intend to use the term "white supremacy" in order to emphasize the role of what can objectively be described as *violence* in maintaining the racial caste system to the present day.

Some (e.g., white liberals) may feel that this emphasis upon acts of physical injury inflicted upon the bodies of people of color oversimplifies a complex and subtle ideological phenomenon. After all, so much of the everyday experience of racism does not reach the point of physical injury. I am sure that this is the case and that physical injury is not the only sort of racialized harm that exists in the world. Nevertheless, I am also sure that when we care to look we find that white supremacist violence permeates our society in myriad different forms which all have in common the fact that they directly injure the bodies of people of color. Why do we pay so much attention to racism's subtler forms and comparatively very little to the blatant violence of white supremacy?

Inadequate health care is a form of violence. Poverty is a form of violence. Homelessness is a form of violence. Getting harassed, beaten, and/or killed by the police is a form of violence. Being incarcerated is a form of violence.

None of these forms of violence are faced *solely* by people of color. Nevertheless, brown and especially black people face each of these realities in great disproportion to whites. We need look no further than such consistently violent outcomes to conclude that our society can accurately be described as white supremacist. Moreover, any institution that facilitates, aids, or abets these violent outcomes by any means whatsoever should also be described as white supremacist. For instance, one of the significant ways in which white liberals facilitate white supremacy is by confining discussions of racial injustice to the circulation and rebuttal of racial epithets, thereby obscuring the underlying and pervasive violence that is white supremacy.

However, though this may sound confusing, please understand that by describing our society and its policies and institutions as white supremacist, *I do not* mean to suggest that this fact is in the real long-term interest of the majority of whites. In an immediate, near-sighted, zero-sum sense it is indeed reasonable and correct to say that whites benefit economically from *both* the fact that they are not subject to systemic caste-based violence and from the fact that people of color routinely are. Moreover, I believe that it is the accurate (albeit myopic) perception of the short-term economic benefits of white supremacist policies that best accounts for the fact that whites in general (and white liberals in particular) have done so little to stop the violence inherent to mass incarceration and the dismantling of the welfare state.

That being said, the long-term economic trajectories of the past 30 years quite clearly demonstrate that middle class whites have themselves paid a quite significant price for the economic and social policies that exacted their greatest violence upon people of color. Middle class whites could maintain the illusion that they were unaffected by the harm done to those they deemed unlike themselves insofar as their access to credit allowed them to self-segregate geographically and occupationally. All the while, whites of nearly all education levels and all but the highest income bracket have seen: real wages decline, health care and college costs explode exponentially, work become increasingly temporary when it is available at all, and transportation costs continually rise. 40% of US household income now goes to housing costs. Even in predominantly white regions, public pensions and municipal budgets are bursting at the seams because permanently low interest rates make it impossible for them to generate their projected revenues; but interest rates must be kept permanently low in order to keep the debt merry go-round spinning. Buoyed over more than three decades by cheap foreign consumer goods, their access to credit, and their comparative advantage in the labor market, it took the absurdly naked elite expropriations of the post-2008 economy to make the majority of whites finally recognize the dramatic consequences of the violently exploitative social and economic policies they tolerated if not actively supported over the same period.

While the economic costs of white supremacy are, in the end, very negative for the vast majority of whites along with everyone else, I nevertheless doubt that conventional short-term economic arguments alone will be sufficient to end white supremacist policies. For one thing, the bulk of the costs wrought by white supremacy are social costs and as such they are often all but invisible in terms of the immediate policy alternatives offered by two white supremacist political parties that share an imaginary model of economic reality in which social costs don't exist. It is above all this political and ideological orthodoxy that need be shattered as soon and as irreparably as possible.

Like so much else that is wrong in our society, the continuation of white supremacist policies is inherently conjoined with the supremacy of short-term, individualistic, zero-sum thinking. If we are to overturn our society's most socially injurious policies, we need to broaden not only our collective thinking but our collective feeling as well. The injuries inflicted upon the poor, the imprisoned, the unemployed, the evicted, the foreclosed, the sick, the anguished, the elderly, and the undocumented make their marks upon us all. The more we cut the social safety net in the effort to save a few pennies from falling into the pockets of people who we are told don't deserve them, the more rents go up and wages go down. All of us live poorer and unhappier lives as a result.

0.2.2   On the Constitution of White Supremacist Institutions

There is little to no consideration herein concerning the socioeconomic and cultural divisions within nonwhite populations. It remains to be seen to what degree an analysis of the function played by white liberals in maintaining white supremacy need be supplemented by an examination of the relationship between white liberals and the black and brown bourgeoisie. While a number of black and brown folk do indeed work in the social institutions that I identify as comprising the core of white liberal ideological influence, for the time being, white liberals do indeed still exert an inordinate influence upon these institutions.

To take the most obvious example, while the lack of ethnic diversity in the media as a whole is quite appalling (e.g., the American Society of News Editors reports that minorities constituted 12.3% of the newsroom workforce in 2012, down from 13.7% in 2006[5]) there is much to indicate that whites constitute an even more dominant influence upon shaping the ideology of these institutions than is suggested by the weight of their numerical supremacy in the total workforce alone. For instance, David A. Graham noted that during the 2012 election season, white reporters wrote 93% of front page election stories, 86% of stories on the economy, 88% of stories on social issues, 93% of stories on foreign policy, and 95% of stories on immigration.[6] It would also be interesting to know the percentages of editors who are white. Interestingly, the ASNE keeps demographic statistics for the newspaper workforce as a whole but not specifically for editors.

While greater representation of ethnic minorities at white liberal institutions would almost certainly improve the ideological diversity of these institutions, careful attention always has to be paid to the degree to which these institutions serve white supremacy regardless of numerical representation. This is a particularly important issue to examine with respect to those white liberal institutions, rare but not unheard of, in which whites constitute a minority of the total workforce, but nevertheless, remain the majority in positions of power and influence (e.g., editors, executives, board members, donors, provosts, deans, administrators, etc.). It is my position that with respect to the influence they exert, such institutions can still, properly, be called "white supremacist."

---

[5] http://asne.org/content.asp?pl=140&sl=129&contentid=129

[6] http://www.theatlantic.com/politics/archive/2012/10/infographic-the-enormous-racial-gap-in-political-reporting/264080/

For this analysis, an institution's influence concerns how and to what degree the institution in question facilitates the entrenchment of white supremacy in society both ideologically and materially, regardless of the ethnic representation internal to the institution. For instance, persons of color may constitute a numerical majority of the officers in a given municipal police force but such an institution can and should still be called "white supremacist" according to the extent to which that institution participates in enacting a broader white supremacist social and economic agenda (e.g., by enforcing laws upon people of color through tactics and to a degree not faced by the vast majority of white populations). As the agents of state violence, the police are only a particularly blatant example of how policies and practices of white supremacy do not necessarily need to be implemented directly by whites, much less those who actively identify as white supremacist. Similar, albeit less dramatic, results often apply in certain university, non-profit, and cultural settings.

In sum, while institutions are in many respects both productive of and produced by the identities of their constituents, nevertheless, we can regard the question of the influence of institutions as an analytically distinct question from that of individual identification. White supremacist institutions could not function, much less to the extent and in the manner that that they do, without incorporating individuals who do not identify as white supremacist.

0.2.3 No Such Thing as the "Working Class"
(without Non-Workers)

I use the term "working class" primarily in order to
signify that portion of the population who are subject
to performing the *more* exploitative forms of labor
within a given society. I use the term "dark working
class" in order to signify the role that whiteness plays
as an exemption—always temporary in nature and
subject to rescission in any given instance—from more
exploitative forms of labor. As should be apparent,
this is a relative definition and thus the constitution of
the group indicated by such a label is always and only
discernible with respect to the particular social system
under investigation. Moreover, and perhaps most
importantly, the question of the interests of the
working class *does not* exhaust the question of social
justice. In fact, the interests of the working class are
only properly maintained for any moment longer than
an instant by the conscious, deliberate, and sustained
amelioration of the material conditions of those who
are not part of the formal labor process.

While I feel that the term working class is useful
for highlighting the exploitative conditions particular
to the portion of society that performs a society's more
exploitative forms of labor, in no way can the
dynamics of class struggle be understood as a direct
result of formal labor relations alone. In many
respects, the conditions of the working class are in
fact determined by the material conditions of those

who are not incorporated within the formal labor force at any given time (e.g., students, the long-term unemployed, the incarcerated, the undocumented, the disabled, the elderly, etc.). While some persons that the state considers outside of the labor force, primarily white, have a temporary exemption from performing more exploitative forms of labor, many others in this category (e.g., the incarcerated and the undocumented) perform *the most* exploitative forms of labor within society. Moreover, many of the most socially essential forms of labor such as child-rearing have always been largely unpaid and informal. It is my view that the traditional labor politics that have attempted to invoke the name "working class" as a banner for class consciousness are doomed to failure until and unless they realize this basic fact: the formal economy would not exist without the informal.

The much heralded phenomenon of globalization—which I take to mean diminished domestic manufacturing related to capitalists and consumers opting for "cheap" goods made possible by the intensified exploitation of foreign workers, themselves often recently displaced from subsistence agricultural economies—does not fully explain the decoupling of worker productivity from wages that has taken place domestically over the last 40 years. While the nature of work has changed significantly, more work than ever is still being done—albeit by fewer workers who are paid less and less for it. Now, of course, elites were behind financing and orchestrating the destruction of the United States middle class but this shouldn't surprise us. The real question is: How were elites so successful at convincing the middle class to collaborate in their own decimation? The irresistibility of consumer culture is at best only a part of the answer and by no means a sufficient one. The War on Drugs, white flight, and the mutilation of the social safety net have everything to do with the servicization, temporarization, and financialization of the US economy that took place over the same period.

When "working class" politics are understood exclusively in terms of the immediate economic interests of workers in the formal sector alone, then the "working class" is an inherently white supremacist and an ultimately self-defeating proposition. The labor movement was all too silent as mass incarceration and its accompanying social ostracization successfully reproduced a racial undercaste all too desperate for work of any kind, under any conditions, and for any pay. They were silent, that is, when they weren't actively collaborating in this fundamentally white supremacist phenomenon. After all, many corrections officers and police are dues-paying union members.

In fact, the means of subsistence available to, and the material conditions applicable to, those persons outside of the formal economy always sets the standard for the wages and conditions of the working class as a whole. The degree to which "non-workers"— to speak metaphorically, for there would be no formal economy without their unpaid labor—*suffer* is the degree to which workers in the formal sector must accept whatever work is thrown their way. It is the suffering of "non-workers" that makes the threats of the elite issued to the working class carry real weight: e.g., a threat to close down a plant, a threat to cut wages, a threat to fire workers who organize, etc. Accordingly, the working class as a whole will only see its modest portion dwindle even further until and unless it secures basic subsistence—not simply in right, but in fact—for every member of society.

In industrialized societies, in which the corporate sector has decided that employment is no longer necessary for the securing of profit, more and more of us will find ourselves without work. The challenge called about by such circumstances—the overriding challenge, which is as immediately personal as it is undeniably global in the nature of its consequences—is to redefine the meaning of work, production, and productivity. Even if you have a job, I guarantee that you know more unemployed people than you did five years ago, and, in all likelihood, that number will only increase. We need a whole range of solutions, adaptations, and innovations to our daily habits, cultural norms, and social institutions. We need to bootleg some shit to get by as best we can as long as we can, and we need to get rid of all the bullshit that says human beings must prove their value in order to get what they need to survive.

The labor movement of the future will look far beyond and far deeper than a campaign for a higher minimum wage. Whatever the minimum wage is in the formal economy—and it is abysmally and inexcusably low at present—the true minimum wage is the much lower rate of so much of the work that goes on in the informal economy which nevertheless makes the formal economy function. Selma James reminds us that the factory system never would have been profitable without the work of women to reproduce the means of production. The bulk of social production never has and never will happen at work (i.e., through formal employment). In light of this fact, the fate of the working class in fact depends upon the institution of a *guaranteed wage* paid *without question* to every member of society. Only when this is its first and last aim can the working class truly be said to be conscious of its own interests.

CHAPTER ONE

*What White Liberals Think of
when They Think of Themselves*

Stuff White People Like
and White Liberal Identity

1.0 Stuff White People Like *and the Search for Satire without Pain*

In this chapter, my aim is to provide an in-depth analysis of the blog Stuff White People Like (hereafter referred to as SWPL) which highlights the fact that the blog's humor fails to reach the level of substantive cultural criticism. SWPL was started in January of 2008 by Christian Lander. The blog describes itself rather concisely as follows: "This is a scientific approach to highlight and explain stuff white people like. They are pretty predictable."
As blogs go, SWPL is remarkably successful: in the 2+ years since going online, it has received over 74 million hits. Building on the success of the blog, SWPL has spawned two books and a day-to-day calendar as well. SWPL has received its share of criticism both in print and via other blogs.[7] However, I believe that thus far this criticism has failed at 1) adequately and clearly explaining the rhetorical mechanism behind what makes SWPL funny and 2) thoroughly and precisely articulating why SWPL's humor fails at fundamentally challenging white

---

[7] Gregory Rodriguez, "White Like Us: A Blogger Explores the Attitudes and Foibles of a New Minority Group," *Los Angeles Times,* February 25 2008. Andrew Battista, "The Problem With "Stuff White People Like"," http://thewellwroughturn.wordpress.com/2008/02/27/the-problem-with-stuff-white-people-like/. Blake Abbot, "How to Win White Friends: Whiteness and Hyper-Visibility in 'Stuff White People Like'," in *National Communication Association Annual Conference* (Chicago, IL: 2009).

privilege. This chapter attempts to address both of these points. Additionally, by providing a clearer conception of how SWPL works and why its humor is not in fact critical of its target (i.e., white people) in any meaningful way, I also hope to offer some suggestions for the kind of cultural analysis that could actually pose a legitimate challenge to white privilege.

Any student of satire knows that the form's success at drawing attention to the problematic aspects of its object can never be guaranteed in advance. In fact, by exaggerating the enjoyment its target produces for the sake of illustrating the absurdity inherent therein, satire is always playing with fire: a caricature which appears absurd and/or monstrous to one person may very well prove to be all the more intoxicating to another. However, as I will explain in greater detail below, the humor of SWPL is a safer game altogether than that of genuine satire. Rather than attempting to make its object seem absurd and/or monstrous—as in the case of Stephen Colbert's depiction of conservatives—SWPL's humor instead functions by mocking its object precisely for its normality, its representativeness, and its harmlessness. SWPL's humor is something safer than satire; because it risks nothing in depicting its object, so there is nothing about that object which its depiction can change. The safety of this humor has indeed made SWPL very popular. However, rather than exposing the real absurdity of white culture—and thus, challenging its readers either to identify with that culture and the injustices which it produces or to disidentify with that culture and to take up the fight against its injustices—SWPL instead chooses to provide one more filter for hiding from view the true grotesqueries of whiteness.

1.1   How SWPL Works

The first time that I saw SWPL, I was somewhat amused in an absent-minded kind of way. However, as I saw more of the things that constitute that category of "stuff" that white people supposedly like, I was a bit confused. Why are things like *Mad Men* and *sushi* listed as "stuff white people like" when such obvious things as NASCAR are not? Is this really accurate? Anecdotally speaking, I probably have as many if not more friends of color who like *sushi* and *Mad Men* as I do white friends. On the other hand, I don't have any friends of any color who like NASCAR (and herein lies the problem with relying upon anecdotal evidence... which is exactly what SWPL does).

Why aren't the staples of white trash culture included within SWPL? The reason for this is simple. The "humor" behind SWPL wholly consists in the fact that it is criticizing a culturally and socially dominant group. This is what makes SWPL's brand of humor safe, inoffensive, and generally palatable, even and especially to white people. Indeed, a more accurate title to SWPL would be: Stuff that People Who Self-Consciously Refer to Themselves as "White" Like. To include things like NASCAR that white people do indeed like—indeed, in the case of NASCAR something that almost exclusively white people like—but that are not seen as desirable by the culture as a whole would challenge the image of white cultural dominance. Without the assumptions that white people are both (a) a monolithic group and (b) a group which is in all cases culturally dominant, SWPL would not be funny at all.

You can see just how much of SWPL's humor hinges upon the fundamental assumption of its group's dominance by a very brief thought experiment. Imagine that someone started a blog called Stuff Red People Like that used a similar voice of pseudo-anthropological description. If such a blog could even exist at all, it would function drastically differently than SWPL for one simple reason: we don't consider Native Americans to be a socially/culturally dominant group and so making fun of them is not a lighthearted affair. It's more like kicking someone who's already down or rubbing salt in the wound or any of those other valuable clichés that we have to express shitting on someone who doesn't deserve it.

And that's exactly what it would sound like if SWPL made fun of the utter vapidity of NASCAR and the uncultured and uneducated idiots who have nothing better to do than watch cars drive hundreds of miles in a circle. Doesn't the last sentence make you cringe just a little bit? That's why SWPL doesn't talk about NASCAR. Somehow, it just feels uncomfortable to make fun of people for liking supposedly lame things when the people being made fun of have no real way of knowing any better. Thus, for the lighthearted humor of SWPL to work, the "stuff" being made fun of cannot be associated with white people who lack education and money—i.e., white people who are not in fact culturally dominant. SWPL can poke harmless fun at white people only by first making sure that the white people it pokes fun at do indeed fit our ideas of what representatives of a culturally dominant group should look like. Otherwise, it would just be uncouth.

Okay, so now we can all agree that SWPL works only because it criticizes a culturally dominant group—namely, the subset of white people who have education and (presumably) money. The next question is, and it's certainly a reasonable one to ask, what's wrong with that? Don't these people who more or less have everything (education + money + white privilege) deserve to be taken down a peg? They certainly do. However, nowhere does SWPL recognize the distinction between the white liberals it makes fun of and the actual white elite. To elide this distinction is to make it difficult if not impossible to understand the way that white privilege actually functions.

1.2   Why SWPL Sucks

Having explicated the assumptions upon which SWPL's brand of safe humor rests, we can now discuss the ways in which SWPL falls short of genuine cultural criticism. In order to be somewhat precise in this analysis, I believe it is helpful to break down the failures of SWPL into three basic categories: 1) *SWPL deliberately misrepresents white culture*; 2) *SWPL makes whiteness seem harmless*; 3) By overcoding cultural values in racial terms, *SWPL makes class politics* all but *invisible*. Now, as we will see, each of these problems is deeply interrelated. However, analyzing each of these problems individually will give us a richer understanding of just how fucked up a whole SWPL is.

1.2.1 SWPL Deliberately Misrepresents White Culture

As I have already discussed above in the course of analyzing the workings of SWPL's humor, it is fairly obvious that SWPL does not in fact represent the cultural tastes of all white people. Its humor manages to come off as innocent rather than openly malevolent only by deliberately focusing on a particular segment of the white population. In fact, the degree to which it does even that is an open question. Does (the) Stuff (that) White People (supposedly) Like really have anything at all to do with whiteness?

Fortunately or unfortunately, the fact is that today people of all different ethnicities, races, religions, nationalities, genders, and sexual orientations like a lot of the same things. Take for instance: *t-shirts, dogs, tea,* and *coffee* (all of which are included in SWPL). By including things of such universal appreciation, SWPL is apparently suggesting that there is a uniquely white way of liking these universal things. That may or may not be the case. However, if the point is really to try to find the distinguishing characteristics of white people's cultural tastes, wouldn't it make more sense to start by cataloging the actual things that white people are disproportionately more likely to like?

The dating website OkCupid has compiled just such a list by analyzing the dating profiles of its white users against those of users of all other ethnicities.[8] Unsurprisingly, OkCupid's list— broken up by gender and based on an analysis of 526,000 user profiles, as opposed to SWPL's free-floating speculation—looks almost nothing like SWPL. The one common element I was able to find between OkCupid's list and SWPL: white women disproportionately like coffee (but not nearly as disproportionately as they like: The Red Sox, Jodi Picoult, boating, NASCAR, mascara, Ireland, Nicholas Sparks, horseback riding, bonfires, or flea markets). Perhaps what's remarkable about the OkCupid list is just how distinct the likes of white men are from those of white women. The two things that white men and white women both disproportionately appreciate are boating and—yep, you guessed it— NASCAR!

It would seem then that boating and NASCAR comprise the very epitome of stuff white people actually like (compared to others) and yet, unsurprisingly, they're nowhere to be found on SWPL. I believe that the very *absence* of these two uber-white

---

[8] Christian Rudder, "The *Real* Stuff White People Like," OkCupid, http://blog.okcupid.com/index.php/the-real-stuff-white-people-like/.

things from SWPL tells us a great deal about the way in which SWPL has drastically curtailed the phenomenon of whiteness to fit its own purposes. If I were to make an analysis of white culture, the contrasting images, lifestyles, and ideologies associated with boating and NASCAR would be the very place from which I would start. As distinct as their cultural connotations are, boating and NASCAR are the two things that white people of both genders like disproportionately over all other groups; these two things are so very different and yet, at the same time, they are both so inescapably and indelibly white. As such, I am tempted to say that boating and NASCAR represent two contrasting polarities of whiteness. The exclusion of these polarities within SWPL constitutes a deliberate attempt to narrow the field of whiteness solely to a group that can be made fun of without any ensuing consequences.

Previously, I suggested that the reason for not including NASCAR on SWPL is that within the culture at large, NASCAR is coded as being a low-status cultural artifact and thus, making fun of it would result in more cringes than chuckles. For the purposes of SWPL's mild-mannered humor, any white people who are poor, uneducated, conservative, and/or religious simply do not count as white. We might even go so far as to say that SWPL's brand of humor enacts a hygienic process upon whiteness. Indeed, part of what makes SWPL funny—if not the very essence of its humor—is that its pseudo-criticism actually functions as a way of whitening up (and, in other cases, whiting out) the real vulgarity of white culture and white people. Even though NASCAR is one of the most disproportionately valued things among actual white people, the people who like it *aren't white enough* for SWPL. In their perceived poverty and ignorance, NASCAR-loving white people just don't do a good enough job of representing what the white race should look like in order to fulfill its status as a dominant group. If NASCAR fans are not white enough to be included in the brand of whiteness that SWPL engineered for the sake of easy inconsequential criticism, then what does the exclusion of boating tell us about that brand? We might say that the predominant cultural image of boating actually makes the people who like it a bit *too white* to be included in SWPL's brand of whiteness.

Of all of the stuff included in SWPL, *living by the water* comes the closest to containing a genuine critique of white social privilege. To include boating, would make such a critique full-blown—and therefore less palatable; as such, boating is not worthy of inclusion. In simple geographic terms, boating does indeed require living in proximity to a body of water. The closer one lives to the water, the less time it takes to get there and thus the more time available for boating; proximity to water is one of the greatest factors in determining both real estate values and population density; living close to water is a scarce commodity that is not accessible to the population as a whole. As such, having access to a body of water sufficient for the sake of boating in and of itself constitutes a position of privilege. All of this is in marked contrast to the considerably cheaper, inland-based, and spectator-driven sport that is NASCAR.

As a leisure activity to be enjoyed on coasts and riversides, many of which neighbor densely-populated post-industrial cityscapes, boating requires significant amounts of disposable time and income: a combination which is restricted to a very select group of people. The people who can afford to own boats for the sake of leisure are often the same people who run things: corporations, businesses, media outlets, legal and medical practices, prisons, government offices, universities, etc. To borrow a phrase from Dave Chappele, we might say that a significant portion of the people who own boats are "the *real* white people." Moreover, whether or not you yourself own a boat, to say that you enjoy boating is in some sense to pledge your cultural allegiance to the white ruling class, regardless of whether or not you yourself are a part of that class. To like boating is to admire the cultural legacy of the bourgeoisie—a legacy passed down through generations of white men. The bourgeois legacy that boating represents consists of not just inherited material privileges like estates and marina leases but also of the sure knowledge that those privileges are to be maintained for your progeny by keeping the dark working class in their place and off your property. The white people who like boating don't have to remind themselves that they're white by reading blogs like SWPL because nearly everything that they have and want—that is to say, nearly everything that defines who they are—is an expression of that fact.

If, as I argued before, SWPL avoids making fun of NASCAR because it is not a representation of cultural dominance, then why does it hesitate to lampoon boating? As an activity, boating is a paradigmatic example of not just cultural dominance but white cultural dominance at that. As such, who could possibly be more deserving of criticism than white people who own boats? Almost no one. And that's the very reason that SWPL does not dissect elite cultural markers like boating: the absurdity, privilege, and ostentation of such things is so very obvious. It's just simply not very funny to point out that people who own boats solely for the sake of leisure tend to be rich, white, boring, self-interested assholes who were given every advantage in the world but who are incessantly paranoid of anyone else having any opportunities whatsoever. No, it's not funny to criticize the *real* white people—it's only true.

The exclusion of on the one hand NASCAR and on the other hand boating effectively sets the parameters for the brand of whiteness that SWPL can poke fun at while still remaining light and inconsequential—i.e., as opposed to serious, important, rude, controversial, confrontational, and/or meaningful. Associating whiteness with things like poverty, lack of education, conservatism, age, wealth, power, patriarchy, religiousness, and cultural closed-mindedness just seems to cut a bit too close to the bone. Now, obviously no white person can be all of these things at once (though he can try!). The point is that by examining whiteness through the polarities represented by NASCAR and boating, we can see the *field* in which white privilege operates; analyzing these contrasting and at times disparate polarities makes the white experience visible in all of its contradictions, complacencies, limitations, excesses, and indulgences. By contrast, constructing a notion of whiteness which deliberately excludes these polarities, as SWPL does, effectively blinds us from understanding whiteness as a unitary socio-cultural field. That is, the negation of white privilege—in the form of the poverty and lack of formal education which are very real factors in the lives of many real white people—is every bit as necessary for its performance, articulation, maintenance, and reiteration as its positive dimension (i.e., wealth, power, status, etc.).

For a variety of reasons, white privilege works not just by othering dark others, but by othering other whites as well. In fact, this is exactly the function that SWPL itself performs by denying both extreme white privilege and underprivileged whites from inclusion. Both must be excluded as to include one would be to suggest the other.

The exclusion of both of these polarities of white privilege is precisely what gives definition to SWPL's brand of whiteness. Accordingly, as far as SWPL is concerned, you are white if and only if you are: middle class (or, more accurately, petit-bourgeois), educated, effete, liberal, young, secular, urban, style-conscious, technologically-adept, non-racist, and open-minded to the art, literature, and cuisine of cultures throughout the world. And, I do indeed mean "if and only if" in the logically formal sense of the biconditional; that is to say, as far as SWPL is concerned, it is meeting these criteria which makes you "white" rather than the color of your skin; as such, the category of "white" is thus projected upon (without any added complication or nuance) to the darker-skinned bourgeoisie as well.

SWPL does indeed do a fairly good job at chronicling the peculiarities of its particular demographic. As a person who more or less fits the designated criteria, I certainly can admit to being amused more than once when SWPL has reflected my own tastes (to name a couple: "sea salt" and "black music that black people don't listen to anymore"). Now, I am certainly not trying to deny that the very specific population examined by SWPL is worthy of criticism. Indeed, I believe this to be the case for all groups and, for that matter, individuals as well. As far as I'm concerned the problem with SWPL is not that it criticizes such people but rather that it fails at doing so robustly and thereby comes off as merely amusing commentary which does nothing to alter the very privilege it lampoons.

A more enduring critique of white petit-bourgeois liberalism would actually emphasize the *continuity* of this group of white people with their redneck and elite brothers and sisters. Viewing white petit-bourgeois liberals in relation to the polarities of NASCAR and boating provides a perspective for an analysis and critique of this group that goes far beyond the mocking yet celebratory treatment they receive courtesy of SWPL. Whatever else they are, white liberals are self-consciously white, so much so that they enjoy websites devoted to the sole purpose of reminding them of that fact. This, in and of itself, attests to the fact that white liberals themselves recognize a continuity between their own whiteness and the transparently vulgar and elite forms of the same phenomenon. This continuity is just patently there, it is something which white liberals are even aware of on a superficial level, and yet they cannot bring themselves to draw the obvious consequences from the fact that they are so intimately related—both literally and figuratively—to both rednecks and the elite. In what does the continuity of whiteness consist? In a word, privilege. However, when privilege is rendered solely as a set of elite cultural values—as it is by SWPL—it seems at best irrelevant and at worst harmless.

1.2.2 *SWPL Makes Whiteness Seem Harmless*

By addressing the dominance of whiteness solely in terms of dominant cultural artifacts—which are by no means unique to white people, incidentally—SWPL makes the structural socioeconomic aspects of whiteness all but invisible. In other words, the self-indulgent, disinterested, disingenuous, and essentially passive humor of SWPL is itself a perfect example of the way in which the power of white privilege often derives from its very invisibility. And this is precisely why SWPL is enjoyable to read: we can partake in poking fun at white people only insofar as we are aware that the white people being made fun of are essentially harmless. Thus, while we can enjoy SWPL only because of the pass it's given for criticizing a dominant group, the effect that it has is precisely that of disarming us to the actual, measurable, quantifiable, and most of all deeply *pernicious* effects of white privilege. No wonder white people like Stuff White People Like so much! That shit is FUBU bitches!

Rather than offering any sort of substantive criticism of the actual *harm* that ideologies and institutions of whiteness cause to real people, SWPL portrays whiteness simply as a state of acquired cultural tastes. Why is whiteness even a problem if all that it means is having a particular taste in music, food, movies and books? Being able to recognize dominant tastes does not in itself serve to identify the socially causal factors which brought those tastes to dominance. Nor does it suggest how the relevant social facts equate to privilege as it is extended to some and not others.

SWPL is in effect a symptom of the very demographic which it lampoons: white liberals. As such, if we are to properly diagnose SWPL—and particularly, the way in which it makes whiteness appear harmless—we must first have a clearer idea of how white liberals fit into the overall landscape of white privilege. One thing to notice concerning the relationship between white liberals and white privilege is how excessively self-conscious the former are of the latter. White liberals frequently deploy self-critical references to their own whiteness and how lame it makes them; many white liberals even routinely go out of their way in order to point out the privileges that they enjoy by virtue of their whiteness. However, in articulating the form which their privilege takes, and SWPL is a perfect example of this, white liberals prefer to utilize cultural terms rather than socio-economic ones. One has the impression from reading SWPL, for instance, that white privilege consists solely in enjoying The Daily Show, foreign films, and ethnic food.

In fact, these tastes are often the result of deeper sociological factors like exposure to an urban lifestyle and/or higher education. True, viewed strictly in terms of these demographic characteristics and the cultural preferences associated therewith, white liberals are indeed a distinct group from rural, uneducated NASCAR fans (who, ostensibly, also enjoy Glenn Beck, Rush Limbaugh, Larry the Cable Guy, etc.). However, do urban living and higher education really in themselves constitute privilege?

The combination of education and urban living does indeed breed petit-bourgeois cultural values like those documented in SWPL. However, it is less clear that this combination can reliably predict *power* and *wealth* as they actually operate today. In their sublime arrogance, white liberals assume that deep down everyone wants what they want—or at the very least that everyone would want those things if certain supposed deficiencies were addressed (i.e., education and diversity of environment). Though white liberals do a wonderful job at guarding themselves from this fact, the truth is that many of the uneducated NASCAR set exert considerably more power over their environment and often even have considerably greater purchasing power (thanks to cheaper rural locales) than they do. All the more reason for white liberals to cling to the elite cultural values that they acquired in school! White liberals might not be able to beat their redneck brethren at either making money or influencing the world around them but at least they know what computers to buy, what movies to watch, and what kind of salt to use! No wonder so many rednecks are simply happy to be rednecks and do not view their cultural status (or lack thereof) as a deficiency to be remedied by white liberal evangelism. Perhaps rednecks know what latte drinkers don't: there is more to privilege in general and white privilege in particular than received elite culture or even the demographic factors which make that reception possible.

If it is irreducible to education, urbanity, and the values learned in those contexts, then what is privilege truly made of? For one thing, genuine privilege is the ability *to make and shape culture*. White liberal "culture"—if it may be so called—is a largely passive affair. Your professor tells you something is true, so you believe it. Jon Stewart recommends a book, so you read it. A celebrity chef cooks a dish on TV and you look for something similar at a fast casual restaurant near you. Obama pledges to make his latest half-measure and you support him. Once more, take SWPL as an example: it doesn't even bother to tell white people what they ought to like. Rather, it functions as a supposedly passive receptor of what white people—in their passivity—just happen to like.

Do white liberals have any outlet in their social lives remotely comparable to the megachcurch? Not only is the megachurch a place where nearly anyone can go to find others willing to help them address their basic human needs: food, shelter, childcare, employment, friendship, conversation, entertainment, intellectual stimulation, etc. Perhaps more importantly, the megachurch is also a place in which nearly anyone can find some way of helping someone else to address similar needs. And, what's more, all of this giving and receiving of social goods takes place for the sake of an overarching purpose: to bring a set of shared beliefs into tangible material form and, in the process, to share those beliefs with still others in the hope that they too might further enrich the community in the future. Now, *that's* privilege.

White liberals *think* that they're privileged but, more often than not, what they suppose to be their "privilege" is in fact merely a set of things they've been given by others—e.g., their cultural tastes, their education, and their desk jobs (while these last). What does the white liberal give and to whom? What does he create and where are its tangible effects? Perhaps he donates some of his rather modest amount of money to a few worthy causes. He has no real effect upon shaping the platforms of said worthy causes. In fact, many of these "causes" exist for the sake of perpetuating themselves as causes. From time to time, if he actually gets out of the shadow of his computer screen(s), a particularly good liberal may be so bold as to volunteer at a soup kitchen—but in no manner does he himself identify with the beneficiaries of this social work, nor does he seek to engage in meaningful, belief-transforming discourse with those whom he is self-righteously helping.

Compared with either rednecks or the boating elite, white liberals live lives that are truly impoverished, in a sense of impoverishment that goes much deeper than the monetary one. While rednecks may or may not have money or status in the society at large, they do have the support of—and more importantly, the opportunity to participate in—a range of traditional cultural institutions: the church, the family, laymen-run civic institutions (e.g., volunteer fire departments, the KKK, etc.), the workplace, etc. On the other hand, white liberals are often: alienated from their elite and/or redneck families, lacking the material resources to support families of their own (particularly given how expensive such an endeavor is when undertaken in urban settings), deeply averse to (or simply too apathetic for) organized religion, and working (or not working) in fields and enterprises (e.g., desk jobs, freelance jobs, creative work) in which they have only minimal contact with either fellow human beings or the natural, physical environment.

As opposed to their redneck brethren, white liberals often share many of the same cultural values—if not always the same political ones—as the boating elite. This should not come as much of a surprise as, after all, petit-bourgeois culture always apes bourgeois culture proper and higher education is the chief means of bourgeois cultural dissemination. However, white liberals do not share with their elite brothers and sisters what truly matters as far as far as genuine cultural privilege is concerned: the ability to participate in the shaping of opinions, beliefs, and values. There is a difference: between going to a university and coming from a family that has a university building named after it, between working at a company and owning one, between looking at a painting in a museum and donating that painting to the museum, between voting—or even campaigning—for a politician and giving enough money to that politician that he or she asks your opinion, between reading political opinion pieces and creating the think tanks which write those pieces.

No wonder white liberals cling so desperately to the token media establishments which cater to reinforcing their pre-existing beliefs—Jon Stewart, Keith Olbermann, Rachel Maddow, NPR, and SWPL. Their secular values, effete temperament, and urban locale effectively prevent white liberals from meaningfully participating in the grassroots cultural institutions of their redneck brethren. At the same time, their lack of access to significant amounts of money and the associated social networks of moneyed people often mean that the vast majority of white liberals are left with no significant way to participate in corporate, governmental, cultural, non-profit, and even academic institutions.

The professoriate—the last niche carved out for white liberals to have a meaningful role in shaping cultural values—is being gradually eliminated in favor of a model of temporary academic employment that is much much less secure and pays much much less than even the majority of other service sector jobs. What let the liberal professoriate play a role in shaping public opinion in the past—on the limited occasions and to the limited extent that they did—was the fact that professors enjoyed a comfortable middle-class income, large amounts of free time apart from their expected duties, a community of other intellectuals to discuss ideas with, a platform for disseminating their ideas (e.g., the classroom, book publishing, print journalism, etc.), and the guarantee (however semi-serious it may have been) that their jobs were secure no matter how controversial were their ideas. For the majority of university instructors today, most of these conditions have significantly eroded if not disappeared entirely. Moreover, increasingly over the past 40 years, academic scholarship (even, and perhaps especially, within the humanities) attained an insularity from other cultural spheres (e.g., journalism, literature, entertainment, etc.) to the point that fewer and fewer professors actually know how to talk in a language that the general public can understand.

Despite these challenges, higher education still often succeeds in disseminating liberal beliefs, opinions, and values to wide swathes of the population. For some reason, studying the humanities and social sciences does seem to instill many students—though by no means all of them—with: the belief that art, literature, and knowledge have value apart from the material resources that may or may not accompany their pursuit; a broader conception of the range of artifacts which constitute art, literature and knowledge; a largely unjustified and perhaps ultimately unjustifiable concern for the well-being of persons beyond those of one's immediate association and; the desire to share these values with others. However, after college is over, there are tragically few places for liberals to go where they can either enact the values they've received or share those values with others.

Web 2.0 culture has been an outlet to be sure—and we would not have the President that we have today without it—but so much of it is based around the closed hermeneutic circle of associating solely with (and, therefore, talking only with) people who already agree with you: i.e., in less fancy terms, "preaching to the choir." The phenomenon of the Tea Party is largely explicable as the cultural and political effects brought by the reception of this same technology (broadband internet service, in particular) in conservative rural areas. The introduction of Web 2.0

social networking has, unquestionably, altered the cultural and political landscape. What is less clear is, firstly, whether these technologies do indeed function as a legitimate check upon the power of elite moneyed interests to shape our beliefs and values and, secondly, whether the constraints of the format (i.e., haltingly brief "status updates") are really sufficient for substantive, value-changing discussion.

To summarize this discussion of the dearth of genuine participatory cultural and social resources pertinent to the lives of white liberals, we can offer the following description. White liberals are: too hip to go to church, too educated to have jobs in which they spend significant amounts of face-to-face time with real people (when they can get jobs at all), too geographically and ideologically insulated to come into frequent contact with people who disagree with them, too distracted by technology and media to sustain encounters with others beyond the exchange of pleasantries, likes, and dislikes (and only rarely expressing reasons for these), too poor to buy cultural influence the way that the elite can, too estranged from their families to derive (intellectual, monetary, and/or emotional) support from them or to contribute (intellectually, monetarily, and/or emotionally) to them, and finally, too poor (both monetarily and culturally) to reproduce themselves and too alienated from their neighbors to create and sustain otherwise durable kinship structures. In sum, for better or worse, white liberals are indeed fairly harmless. That is to say, generally speaking, their lives lack the basic capacities necessary for directly affecting and influencing the course of the world around them and the beliefs and values of the fellow creatures with whom they associate. As such, their ability to harm others directly is about as negligible as their ability to provide meaningful assistance to others in their attempts to better the terms of their lives.

In all of nature, has there ever been a creature less capable of directly affecting the relevant facts of its existence than the modern American white liberal? When left to themselves, white liberals simply do not know how to: grow their food, fix their cars, take care of their children (if they're lucky enough to have children in the first place), build their computers, share their beliefs (in terms that their fellow creatures can understand), give appropriate thanks to nature for all that it provides, or help their fellow creatures in procuring life's necessities. They can, however, make some really snarky remarks on Facebook.

We might ask, biologically speaking, how does such a creature manage to exist at all? If left to their own devices, white liberals would have died out long ago. Somehow, despite their inherent passivity, they do indeed manage to survive. This fact, in and of itself, constitutes the distinctive nature of the form of white privilege that is particular to white liberals. They are perhaps the only creatures in the history of the world who have found a way to exist without having to either: 1) procure their material necessities or 2) directly exploit others who procure those necessities. How do they do it?

In fact, they don't. Obviously, such a feat is a strict biological impossibility. And yet, the very fact that white liberals can *appear* to pull off this feat—living without either having to work or to connive others into working for them—tells us something very important about the actual conditions of their survival: white liberals are not in themselves a distinct political community. They are able to survive without significantly contributing to the material, technological, and infrastructural resources upon which their survival depends for one reason and one reason alone: they have been granted a special dispensation by those who actually control the production and distribution of material resources. In the biological world, nothing is given without a reason. If elites allow white liberals to exist—and what's more to exist in an economic position in which they are slightly removed from more exploitative forms of labor—there must be some discernible benefit that their existence provides to the elite.

White liberals are useful to the government-running, business-owning, university-endowing elites as a protective buffer between themselves and the dark working class (not to mention NASCAR loving rednecks as well). The function of white liberals—the purpose that legitimates their existence—is that of providing an explanation for the fact that the few have so much more than the many. Whether or not white liberals actually contribute to producing ideological justifications for inequality, *the very fact of their existence is in and of itself a justification of elite power.*

White liberals provide a visible example of a harmless, easy, apathetic, ostensibly enjoyable, consumption-driven existence which is largely free from both actual physical labor and the marshaling of force necessary for reaping profits from the physical labor of others. This example (i.e., white liberals) is useful to elites for a number of reasons. First, the inconsequential and (relatively) harmless existence of white liberals makes it appear as if the benefits of elite culture extend to a much larger group than they actually do. Because they ape elite tastes in music, art, books, and movies, and because they don't really have to work for a living, white liberals *seem* to live like we imagine that elites live (perhaps the only real thing separating appearance and reality in this case is the fact that, as opposed to elites, white liberals have no real power in shaping the facts of their lives). Second, free as it largely is from productive labor, the "privileged" lifestyle of white liberals stands as a goal or dream that can be sold to the dark working class (and white rednecks) as a means of ensuring their complacency within an elite-dominated economic system. The dark working class and poor rednecks are told: be good, and maybe, just maybe, some day you too can go to college and you'll no longer have to remember how to feed yourself or how to talk to the rest of your family. Third, white liberals provide a convenient target for the dark working class (and poor rednecks) to blame for the fact of their enslavement (rather than this blame being directed at those who are most directly responsible for that enslavement and who benefit from it most robustly, i.e., the elites).

Now, finally, we can at last see the true form of privilege that is unique to white liberals. Their privilege most certainly does not consist in their passive consumption of particular books, movies, TV shows, and food. Nor does it consist in the largely impotent role they play in "raising consciousness" for humanitarian political causes. Nor does it consist solely in their exemption from more exploitative forms of material labor. Nor does it even truly consist in their greater opportunities to pursue higher education and live in highly-desired locations. White liberals do indeed have a genuine role to play in shaping culture. They perform this role not so much by what they say but simply by being themselves: inconsequential, ironic, amusing, hedonistic, apathetic, disinterested, cynical, dispassionate, self-conscious, self-centered, self-critical, self-reflexive, self-important consumers. The more they fit this role, the more complete their performance, the more effective is their exercise of white privilege. The distinctive contribution of white liberals to the overall functioning of white privilege can be summed up as follows: their role is to convince the world that rich people don't exist—or at the very least, that they are not the biggest problem facing the world today.

White liberals, in their comfortable, harmless, and inconsequential existence, provide a living, breathing excuse for both: 1) the staggering, astronomical, odious, criminal, deeply violent amounts of wealth that end up in the hands of rich people (most of whom are white) and 2) instances of white supremacist violence perpetrated against darker skinned peoples by elites and their redneck operatives. The relative exemption which white liberals receive from material labor makes it appear that the spoils of wealth are spread much farther than they are in actual fact, i.e., much farther than elites are willing to let them spread. Similarly, if it does nothing else, the existence of white liberals makes it appear—including to white liberals themselves—that white people aren't all homicidal (if not genocidal) maniacs who will take your life in a heartbeat for a reason as simple as that they lack another better form of entertainment at a given moment (to say nothing of those instances in which homicide and/or genocide might very well be immensely profitable). Rather than examining their role in furthering white supremacist violence and the immense economic inequalities that go hand-in-hand with white supremacist violence, white liberals would rather analyze the shortcomings of their own tastes in music and movies.

SWPL is a perfect example of how white liberals' self-obsession prevents them from recognizing the real harm caused by white privilege (including in the form of their own self-obsession). SWPL manufactures an image of white people as effete, educated, liberal and essentially harmless—thereby, the actual violence done by white people becomes all but invisible. Viewed from SWPL, the power of white privilege means nothing more than a particular set of bourgeois tastes that have no obvious connection to economic, governmental, corporate, and civic structures of oppression. In the world of SWPL, white privilege amounts to little more than liking petit-bourgeois shit, and this itself appears as a value which seems to come from nowhere. What is perceived as coming from nowhere suggests no obvious means of being undone. This is why poking fun at "white people" is such innocent fun—it's essentially harmless, just like the (false) image of the people being made fun of. Seriously, *real* white people have guns, yo. And if they themselves don't have guns, the people that do have them are usually on their side (e.g., the police). There is no such thing as white privilege that is not supported by either (a) white supremacist violence and its ensuing fear or (b) racist institutional policies and outcomes (usually made possible by [a]).

SWPL presents harmless white liberals as a species unto themselves and what's even worse makes this imaginary species stand for the category of whiteness as a whole. As we have seen, white liberals are in fact intimately related to both rednecks and the elite—none of these groups could exist without one another. That is to say, by presenting a harmless image that stands for all white people and thus making the image of white supremacist violence disappear, white liberals are fundamentally necessary for legitimating that violence and thereby ensuring its continued performance. SWPL is one instance—and a particularly blatant one—of the function white liberals play in securing, engendering, and enacting white privilege for themselves as well as for rednecks and the elite.

1.2.3   SWPL Makes Class Politics Invisible

Many of the cultural artifacts which SWPL chronicles have at least as much to do with class-based privilege as they do with race-based privilege. Take the following stuff for instance: *Manhattan, architecture, living by the water, graduate school, gentrification, study abroad, lawyers, the Ivy League.* These are all things associated with the economic elite—or at least with people who aspire to throw in their lot with the elite. However, SWPL treats artifacts of economic privilege like these as being reducible to cultural preferences alone—as if there were no deeper socioeconomic factors responsible for white people having disproportionate access to such artifacts.

Obviously, class-based privilege and race-based privilege are intimately linked. One of the most pernicious ways in which white privilege operates is by guaranteeing that white people have disproportionate access to economic opportunities while denying similar opportunities to others. Similarly, given the preexisting and ongoing disparities in socioeconomic status among racial groups, white privilege often no longer needs explicit race-based discrimination in order to perpetuate itself: a strikingly similar result can often be achieved by relying upon systems of economic discrimination alone. Thus, by erasing the dimension of class differentiation as a point of analysis within white privilege, SWPL effectively insures that: 1) one of the most central social mechanisms through which white privilege operates and perpetuates itself is rendered invisible and 2) white people are reduced to a monolithic group in which all members share equally in its privilege regardless of their socioeconomic status.

As a consequence of relying upon an analysis of race-based privilege which is purely cultural—rather than cultural *and* socioeconomic—SWPL renders a deeply misleading image of society in which class-based privilege seemingly does not exist. Or, if it does exist within SWPL, then class privilege is only an extension of race privilege and therefore something—presumably—shared equally by all white people. By treating white people not just as a monolithic group but as one in which only middle-class white liberals exist, SWPL effectively insures that it is impossible to recognize the distinction between—for instance—the petit-bourgeois pretensions of white liberals and *the actual class privilege* wielded by the rich. In SWPL's world, rich people simply don't exist and poor people only exist insofar as white liberals appropriate—and/or distance themselves from—their culture.

So much of the humor of SWPL depends upon an implicit—and ultimately inaccurate—conflation of white liberals with the elite. At the same time, as I argue above, SWPL cannot fully commit to designating whiteness as an essentially elite phenomenon and so it doesn't include things like: boating, yachts, hedge funds, trust funds, vacation homes, private jets, expensive cars, Swiss (or Singaporean or Cayman) bank accounts, etc. White people's disproportionate access to these artifacts is not worth drawing attention to simply because the (economically-derived) privilege inherent in such artifacts is so transparently absurd that it is nearly impossible to caricature. Drawing attention to such artifacts and the ridiculously small number of people who have them is not so much humorous as it is serious. Thus, for the sake of preserving its ineffectual humor—which is, after all, the factor most responsible for its popularity—SWPL restricts itself to analyzing the cultural artifacts through which white liberals attempt to associate themselves with the elite rather than the cultural artifacts that are in themselves definitive signs of accomplished membership within the elite.

Our analysis concerning the manner in which SWPL makes class politics invisible by conflating white liberals' cultural preferences with actual class privilege is nearly complete. This conflation is indeed the overarching—and as we will discuss below, deeply pernicious—effect produced by SWPL's reduction of society to cultural artifacts and its reduction of white privilege to white liberalism (thanks to a deliberately misrepresentative sample of white cultural artifacts). However, there is one other interesting feature worth pointing out concerning the manner in which SWPL makes this deeply inaccurate conflation of white liberal pretension with actual class privilege.

In addition to including things that white liberals have and or do in order to associate with the elite, SWPL also includes many references to things that white people associate with precisely in order to distance themselves from the elite. For example: *political prisoners, picking their own fruit, free healthcare, camping, ugly sweater parties, music piracy,* and *t-shirts.* For SWPL, this seeming contradiction in the cultural values of its target population (white liberals) regarding elite vs. anti-elite tastes is easily resolved by resorting to a facile—and indeed self-referential—interpretation: when white liberals like aspects of anti-elite culture, they do so with a sense of *irony.* This is made all the more clear by the entry on irony included within SWPL:

> White people hate a lot of stuff (white people who vote republican, television, Vin Diesel movies, SUVs, fast food) but every once in a while they turn that hate into sweet irony.... But the reason that white people love irony is that it lets them have some fun and feel better about themselves.

The implications of this passage are clear: 1) white liberals are the only white people who count (e.g., as opposed to "white people who vote Republican" or those who drive SUVs), 2) whenever white people (read: white liberals) like something that appears to go against their elite cultural pretensions, they are only doing so out of a sense of *irony*. As a consequence of the latter assumption, white liberals can never be considered as genuinely disavowing their association with the elite *no matter what they do*. Thus, according to this perspective, by ironically (i.e., disingenuously) appropriating anti-elite cultural artifacts, white liberals are in fact only providing another brand of evidence for their overall status as members of the elite.

It is true, in recent years, an entire subculture has indeed sprung up in which the practice of disingenuous ironic appropriation of anti-elite (often white trash) cultural artifacts is a measure of cultural capital: members of this subculture have become known as "hipsters." Though one of the distinguishing characteristics of hipsters is their refusal to self-identify as "hipsters," nevertheless, an empirically-observable consensus has emerged regarding the cultural markers of food, dress, transportation, and lifestyle which set the hipster subculture's unique parameters. Moreover, regardless of the manner in which hipsters self-identify, for many, these parameters of acceptable cultural artifacts are adhered to with a near religious level of precision. A hipster would no sooner be caught wearing slacks and loafers than a WASP would go to church in a t-shirt. Even the laziest observer could not help but notice the expanding prevalence of anti-elite cultural artifacts (e.g., tattoos, cheap tasteless beer like Pabst Blue Ribbon and Miller High Life, analog rather than digital music devices, homemade clothes or clothes that appear to be homemade, delicacies of redneck cuisine like frito pie, bikes rather than cars, etc.) among young people residing in post-industrial urban centers such as San Francisco's Mission District and Brooklyn's Williamsburg (to cite the two most obvious examples). Just as the SWPL entry suggests, disingenuous *irony* is indeed often characteristic of the manner in which hipsters—who are above all else a subset of white liberals—deploy these anti-elite cultural artifacts. While hipsters may dress like rednecks, enjoy (old) redneck music, eat redneck food, and drink redneck beer, they still expect you to know that they're not actually rednecks. Hipsters appropriate numerous redneck cultural artifacts, but they are entirely unwilling to go all the way in identifying with the sociologically deeper aspects of redneck culture. It is precisely the deeper aspects of redneck culture that hipsters refuse to appropriate—e.g., family values, rural living, white supremacist violence, and church-going—which constitute the genuine, participatory white privilege that rednecks enjoy (as opposed to the derivative and passive white privilege of hipsters and other white liberals). Like the rest of white liberals, hipsters generally like their culture better when they don't have to pay dues for it.

Clearly, there is much to criticize about hipsters' sociologically detached use of cultural artifacts. From the vantage of SWPL, the hipster appropriation of redneck cultural artifacts is characteristic of the manner in which white liberals often attempt to deny their association with the elite. This denial of eliteness on the part of white liberals is in turn interpreted as a form of negation in the Freudian sense (*Verneinung*)—i.e., a formal denial which actually affirms the very content it attempts to deny. However, as tempting as this analysis is, there is above all one crucial fact which it overlooks (and, in fact, performatively conceals): *white liberals are not the elite.*

SWPL's entry on *irony* does indeed touch on the problematic disingenuousness of hipster culture. The deeper irony is that SWPL's mocking assessment of white liberal privilege suffers from the very disingenuousness which it mocks. SWPL lacks any real critical power vis-à-vis hipsters or other white liberals—and thus, is itself nothing more than an ironic appropriation—because it refuses to allow space for the possibility that there are actual things that white liberals can do that have the potential to confront elite privilege. SWPL gives the impression that *any* attempt by hipsters or white liberals to side with anti-elite cultural values is *a priori* disingenuous.

When we assume from the outset that anything white liberals do to resist their association with the elite is disingenuous, then we have effectively prevented ourselves from seeing their behavior in any other light. In turn, there is no way of evaluating the difference between ironically appropriating anti-elite cultural artifacts on the one hand and actual political activism on the other. Admittedly, there are problems with white liberal activism in its various forms, but the most essential of these is that that activism fails to confront elite class privilege. Mocking someone simply for trying—however ineffectively—to confront class privilege does not by itself encourage other more successful attempts to confront that privilege. In fact, in all likelihood, it has precisely the opposite effect: it suggests that there is no legitimate reason whatsoever for confronting the inequality of wealth which is the cornerstone of our society's violence.

This refusal to take seriously the fact that rich people do indeed exist—and that even if they espouse "liberal" political views, they have no real connection to the social, cultural, and economic contradictions which mark the lives of white liberals—is the essence of SWPL's humor. The widespread acceptance of the idea—really, the ideology in the technical sense of the term—that resistance to elite privilege on the part of white liberals is necessarily and automatically disingenuous actually functions as a self-fulfilling prophecy. In other words, not only is SWPL merely a passive chronicle of disingenuous white liberal anti-elite activism; by insisting upon the ubiquity of this disingenuousness, and having itself become a fixture of white liberal culture, SWPL actually plays a role in guaranteeing precisely that result. The more it is automatically assumed that white liberals are always and necessarily disingenuous whenever they associate with anti-elite values, the more difficult it becomes to draw *the actual* distinction between white liberals and the *real* white people (i.e., the rich).

1.3   *Making the Invisible Visible: The Difference between White Liberals and the Elite*

The analysis of the three most problematic aspects of SWPL's brand of humor that I previously identified is now complete. To summarize: First, by letting white liberals stand as the exclusive representatives of white privilege, SWPL hides both rednecks and the elite from view. Second, this misrepresentation of the spectrum of whiteness prevents us from seeing the real harm caused by white supremacist institutions and policies. Thirdly, SWPL portrays white privilege as a phenomenon that is socioeconomically flat and static—rather than as the differentiated and dynamic socioeconomic phenomenon that it actually is—and thus renders invisible the distinction between those with received petit-bourgeois cultural preferences (i.e., white liberals) and those who actually have the power to shape elite culture (i.e., the rich).

When we only look at white liberals as representative beneficiaries of white privilege and fail to see them within the context of the larger social, political, and economic community to which they belong, we fail to understand the essential function they perform within the maintenance and reproduction of white privilege. Also, by carrying a socially and economically myopic view of white liberals—in which we attempt to analyze their privilege purely in cultural terms alone—we also fail to understand the truly essential quality of whiteness as it relates to cultural privilege. This is the essential error made by SWPL. By suggesting that the values and tastes which it observes can be described primarily if not exclusively as the expression of racial culture, SWPL thereby fails to place these values and tastes in proper social and economic perspective, and thus, SWPL also misses the truly racially-biased character of even the very cultural phenomena it observes. White people don't just live by the water because something peculiar about their culture makes them enjoy living by the water. They like to live by the water because they can afford to and they can afford to largely because of the benefits that they continue to receive from historically white supremacist institutions.

Undoubtedly, SWPL is by no means the only cultural artifact to offer similarly illusory (and similarly problematic) portrayals of white privilege. If it seems that I have been unduly harsh and critical in my analysis of what is only a humorous blog—albeit a very popular one—this was not entirely without reason or justification. As a pristine document of white liberal self-obsession, SWPL provides a deeply revelatory lens with which to view the social function played by white liberals as a whole (and their representative cultural artifacts: NPR, Stewart, Colbert, Olbermann, Maddow, etc.). In sum: the existence of white liberals is one of the main things that keep us from realizing that the rich are much, much more than merely a part of our social problems. The violence inherent to today's unfathomably unequal (and historically unprecedented) distribution of resources is *the* single greatest problem in the world. White liberals play a part in perpetuating that violence because, above all else, they encourage us to forget that rich people exist. In their self-obsession, white liberals make wealth and the wealthy seem invisible (especially to them).

To be truly rich, it seems from the perspective of white liberal cultural artifacts like SWPL, is to be so white as to be invisible entirely. Invisibility is the greatest gift that the rich could ever receive. In fact, it is the thing which they desire more than anything in the world with the possible exception of money. Invisibility is what allows the rich both to keep their money and to do whatever they want with it without any regard for the interests of the vast majority of people on the planet. If we knew there were rich people, and we knew where they lived, we could ask them for money. We could show them our suffering. We could tell them what we expect them to do about it. We could make them think twice about taking everything that we make and leaving us with nothing. The rich know this and that's why they prefer to remain invisible. White liberals are the cloak of invisibility manufactured and worn by the rich. Too often, in only being able to see themselves, even white liberals forget that the rich exist. White liberals certainly forget—if they could ever see it in the first place—that, just by being themselves, they are exactly what allows the elite to be as rich as they are.

CHAPTER TWO

A Social Ecological Account of the White Liberal

2.0   Limbo as the Defining Condition of the White Liberal

In the previous chapter, I roundly and exhaustively criticized *Stuff White People Like* for failing to confront the socioeconomic nature of the cultural phenomena that it lampoons. However, when the cultural phenomena detailed by SWPL are viewed from a deep, naturalistic, and socioeconomically informed perspective, they do indeed shed light upon the unique place played by white liberals in the maintenance of white supremacy and economic exploitation. While SWPL's analysis of this group is both myopic and non-confrontational, the very notion of looking at white liberals as a distinct group—indeed, a species unto themselves—is an idea which has the potential to yield many genuinely robust insights for a critique of the dominant institutions of privilege that SWPL itself only ends up celebrating.

At first glance, the existence of white liberals appears as an essentially contingent phenomenon. As I argue above, they perform no immediately obvious material function necessary for the maintenance and reproduction of society. So much of the world is simply separated into the rich and the poor and never the twain shall meet. I don't exactly know how, but somehow, in the West, there evolved this truly peculiar historical phenomenon of the white liberal—a creature which, on the one hand, shares many of the cultural values of the rich (while being systematically barred from sharing in the real social and economic privileges afforded to the rich) and, on the other hand, still maintains a sentimental fondness for the well-being of the dark poor (a sentiment which, generally speaking, lacks any operative means for altering the actual distribution of material resources). What a truly remarkable aberration! What a truly invaluable case for scientific study! Natural science progresses in its understanding of the most dominant, normal, healthy, and common forms of phenomena only by examining those typical cases in relation to the atypical cases of freaks, pathologies, diseases, exceptions, and abnormalities. The white liberal is just such an evolutionary freak and should be studied accordingly—and for the benefit of all humankind.

Biologically speaking, the demarcation of the point at which one species begins and another ends is always a somewhat arbitrary matter. In absolute terms, the question of what separates one group from another is as undecidable as the question of whether a truly closed system (e.g., a language, logic, program, economy, machine, organism, ecology, etc.) is possible. That is to say, decisions of categorical classification often emphasize the differences between arbitrarily-assigned groups at the expense of deemphasizing the often equally immense genetic and/or environmental differences that exist within the members of any single grouping. As such, the accuracy of the demarcation of a given species (or any other naturalistic group) should be judged *not only* with respect to its descriptive accuracy, but ultimately, with respect to the usefulness of such a demarcation for understanding the broader field of environmental activity. In other words, most fundamentally, the question of natural demarcation is *not* that of whether or not a given selection of individuals constitutes a biologically distinct grouping—indeed, the notion of a "biologically distinct grouping" is *always* an essentially problematic one in biology.[9] Thus, the fundamental question of natural demarcation is instead: *how does viewing this species as a distinct group help us to understand the organization of activity present in the overall environment being observed?*

On the basis of this criterion, the decision to classify the white liberal as a distinct species can only be justified *retroactively* insofar as such a demarcation provides a richer account of the organization of the field of socioeconomic activity than would be possible otherwise. The fact that the continued existence of the white liberal depends upon both the genetic and economic contributions of other distinct groups (and intra-species diversity as well) in no way suggests that such a classification is inaccurate. Rather, this fact itself comprises an essential point of departure from which our biological analysis of the white liberal can properly begin. We can learn a great deal about the white liberal by examining the ways in which this species depends upon and relates to others—e.g., the dark working class, rednecks, and the rich. This in turn will allow us to examine the function that white liberals perform with respect to the dominant organizational structures of the field of socioeconomic activity in which they find themselves: capitalism and white supremacy.

---

[9] For a detailed account of the ways in which supposedly distinct species have much more to do with each other than we generally assume, see: Sean B. Carroll, "Hybrids May Thrive Where Parent Species Fear to Tread," *New York Times*, September 13 2010.

When viewing the white liberal as a distinct species which exists as a function of the natural environment, the first thing that becomes apparent about this species is that its material existence is constituted by a multi-dimensional state of *limbo*. As we shall see, the condition of limbo—of being betwixt and between, neither here nor there, neither this nor that—is constitutive of the white liberal economically, socially, and cultural. Of course, all of these forms of white liberal limbo are intimately and inextricably linked just as economic, social, and cultural facts always are. However, as we shall see below, we can gain a better understanding of the white liberal's multi-dimensional limbo by analyzing these dimensions of experience more or less discretely.

2.1 *The Cultural Limbo of White Liberals*

As consumers, white liberals have a fairly extensive appreciation for the world's diversity of cultural artifacts. However, they themselves rarely *participate* in culture in any meaningful sense. When they do engage in cultural work, their "culture" is *almost never* a thorough-going, organic, and holistic outgrowth of their lifestyle, worldview, social conditions, economic circumstances, beliefs, values, and opinions. Similarly, their cultural works are almost always produced for the sake of an audience of mere consumers rather than one of co-creators. Of course, there are subcultures affiliated with white liberals to varying degrees (e.g., gay culture) that serve as exceptions to the shallow, non-participatory nature of white liberal culture in general. However, with respect to the movies, music, TV shows, books, and cuisine that make up the bulk of the canon of white liberal culture, it is indeed accurate to characterize these works as neither deep (i.e., expansively engaged with the whole of life, particularly material struggle) nor participatory.

This detached, superficial relationship to cultural artifacts arises largely out of the white liberal's unique socioeconomic conditions. In the final analysis, white liberal privilege—in the genuine, participatory sense of the word—extends to the rather modest talents the species has acquired for ensuring their continued place of limbo within elite-dominated society. As we will further discuss the terms of the white liberal's position of social and material limbo below: the white liberal knows very well that his position is inherently precarious, that any misstep could lead the rich to rescind his exemption from the most exploitative forms of labor (which is the chief condition necessary for his continued existence). How does the white liberal hold onto his existentially-defining exemption? Primarily, by doggedly learning the tastes, values, beliefs, and ideologies of the elite—what is called, in a word, *education*. It is this drive towards education—out of all proportion to the career prospects which it engenders and the costs and debts which it requires—which is the single most distinguishing aspect of the white liberal. The habituated skills that the white liberal accrues in pursuit of education constitute his greatest measure of privilege in the genuine sense of the word.

Before we proceed, let me say a bit about what education means in this robust socioeconomic context. By education, I mean the sum total of governmental, corporate, non-profit, ecclesiastical, and informal institutions and mechanisms of patronage which exist primarily for the sake of deciding who receives an exemption from the more exploitative forms of labor and who does not. This definition would include all of the various forms of taught education at all different levels, but it would include many other things as well. For instance, it would also include tutoring and test preparation, the body of supplemental theoretical and practical wisdom necessary for success in taught educational institutions but not included directly in those institutions (this supplemental wisdom is largely disseminated through families and to a lesser extent through informal networks), athletic institutions at all different levels (esp. as these interface with taught education), and, finally, legal and penal institutions (as the most effective and immediate mechanism for rescinding exemptions from exploitative labor). This definition of education would exclude institutions which disseminate knowledge without any potential impact concerning who gets to do what kinds of work. Workshops in non-marketable skills and crafts should probably be excluded, as should any formal or informal education geared toward seniors (whose fate as laborers has largely already been determined). The fact that it is easier to specify institutions that do *not* conform to this definition of education (rather than to specify those institutions which do) indicates the ubiquity of the determinative function we are talking about.

Education, in the sense in which we are talking about it, is a sorting mechanism. Its purpose is to codify, reinforce, and justify intended disparities between the social and economic opportunities afforded to white liberals and those afforded to rednecks and the dark working class. When looking at the matter objectively and apart from the comparatively insignificant issue of the content knowledge that is or isn't disseminated in the process, this is exactly the function performed by any and all educational institutions.

Thus far, I have spoken of the social function of education with respect to white liberals. Understanding this social function is necessary for adequately encountering what I promised to explain in this section: the manner in which the unique place afforded to white liberals in educational institutions becomes the basis for white liberal culture. First, we can say (accurately but not exhaustively) that the culture imparted to white liberals in the course of education is elite culture. Preferring wine to beer, books to TV, foreign or independent movies to Hollywood are tastes that can be seen as clear remnants of the leisure-based bourgeois conception of culture. However, unlike the rich, white liberals cannot significantly shape the aesthetic values and distinctions which determine their world of cultural artifacts; they have leisure but not capital and as such they are, for the most part, doomed to recapitulate a degraded form of the tastes of the elite. Essentially, this is the cultural limbo of white liberals: they have the resources to consume but not the resources to shape, in a significant way, either the objects which they consume or the terms of their own consumption.

By claiming that the cultural position afforded to white liberals is above all that of a consumption-driven relationship to quasi-elite culture, I do not mean to suggest that white liberals respond to this situation in a univocal way. Yes, some white liberals not only recognize that they receive their tastes from the elite but openly proclaim that fact. However, shame, apathy, and resentment are just as common (if not, indeed, more common) ways for the white liberal to respond to his position of cultural limbo. Still, these forms of cultural disavowal often, though not necessarily, evidence an unwitting acceptance of the aesthetics and tastes pioneered by the elite. This connection was made quite explicit in a famous speech from the film *The Devil Wears Prada* in which a fashion magazine editor eloquently reproaches her assistant for claiming that the elite-dominated fashion industry was irrelevant to her life:

> You go to your closet and you select out
> — oh, I don't know — that lumpy blue
> sweater, for instance, because you're trying
> to tell the world that you take yourself too
> seriously to care about what you put on your

back. But what you don't know is that that
sweater is not just blue, it's not turquoise,
it's not lapis, it's actually <u>cerulean</u>. You're
also blithely unaware of the fact that in
2002 <u>Oscar de la Renta</u> did a collection of
cerulean gowns. And then I think it was
<u>Yves St. Laurent</u>, wasn't it, who showed
cerulean military jackets? (I think we need a
jacket here). And then cerulean quickly
showed up in the collections of eight
different designers. Then it filtered down
through the department stores and then
trickled on down into some tragic <u>Casual
Corner</u> where you, no doubt, fished it out of
some clearance bin. However, that blue
represents millions of dollars and countless
jobs and it's sort of comical how you think
that you've made a choice that exempts you
from the fashion industry when, in fact,
you're wearing a sweater that was selected
for you by the people in this room.[10]

The magazine editor is quite right in pointing out
that it is often the elite who produce the cultural
values which the rest of us come to take for granted.
However, the assistant's disavowal of her own
participation in elite culture is also a quite
understandable response: can those of us who fail to
take an interest in high fashion really be blamed when
we have nowhere near the material resources that
such an active interest would require? Hence, the

---

[10] David Frankel, "The Devil Wears Prada," (United States: 20th
Century Fox, 2006).

situation of cultural limbo which white liberals face: their exemption from the most exploitative forms of labor allows them just enough material comfort in order to consume degraded forms of elite culture, but, unlike the rich, they do not shape elite cultural values.

2.1.1   The White Liberal on Vacation

I believe that the best way to illustrate the cultural limbo of white liberals is by telling a story. Let us tell of what happens when the white liberal goes on *vacation*. First we should say that we see the word "vacation" as the name for a phenomenon which is more expansive than the strict circumstances to which the term is generally applied. The meaning of a *vacation* is any moment in which a white liberal mistakenly attempts to participate directly in elite culture. These moments are as tragic as they are unavoidable. Having been educated to appreciate elite culture, and always noticing (and often exaggerating) his differences with the dark working class, it is unavoidable that the white liberal will at some point attempt to engage with elite culture in some manner. Such moments are tragic because, try as he might, the white liberal simply cannot afford it. One might say that the moment of vacation that we will attempt to describe serves as a metaphor for the more impalpable process of education as a whole.

The white liberal's vacation among the elite takes on a fairly melancholy tone. Unlike members of the dark working class, he can indeed pass among the elite, but only for a limited time and under the threat of bankruptcy. Of course, passing always comes with both its rewards and its risks, and often, these come in an indivisible package. When the white liberal first tastes the spoils of elite privilege, he is overcome with a feeling of uncanny familiarity. His education, if not the entirety of his upbringing and social existence, has taught him to value the artifacts of elite culture—the right paintings, music, art, and cuisine. And now, here he is, at last, on vacation in the presence of the rich, actually experiencing these things for himself for the first time, as opposed to hearing third-hand accounts of their supposed virtues. A decidedly queer feeling comes upon seeing an original painting that one knows from books on display in a rich person's private residence. No less queer is the feeling of finally tasting a meal at the famous restaurant that one has read about at great length in books, magazines, and online review websites. In preparation for such a vacation, not only does the white liberal set aside a significant portion of his current (or future) income; with nearly just as much dedication, the white liberal does his homework. He knows what to order, how to say a few words in French, and not to act too excited regardless of how delighted he is with the experience. Above all, he wants to act like he belongs—after all, that desire is the reason that the white liberal goes on vacations in the first place.

However, these vacations come to the white liberal at a considerable cost; the great material expense of the vacation leads to a second deeply spiritual expense. The pleasure the white liberal finds in experiencing the uncanny objects of elite culture is accompanied by an equally immediate sensation of pain. The food tastes better than even the image of it conjured from reading its celebratory reviews; the painting looks even more beautiful from up close where the brush strokes can be made out. And yet, the very sublimity of the experience is precisely what reminds the white liberal of the fact that the objects which he enjoys for this fleeting instant are not truly his to enjoy. He could never afford to eat like this every day any more than he could afford to have such a painting in his apartment. Finally, for the white liberal, having access to elite objects only serves to remind him of the limits and conditions under which that access is granted; the temporary and fleeting presence of these objects during a moment of vacation accentuates the fact that under normal circumstances, in the course of his real everyday life, such objects are definitively beyond his reach. Paradoxically, it is the elite object's very *presence* which makes the white liberal's experience of it one of melancholy, in a way that longing for it from afar never could.

Thanks to his complexion and its complimentary ideology of Invisibility, the white liberal is used to feeling welcome wherever he goes. This wonderfully optimistic ideology teaches the white liberal to think of himself as a person like any other, no better or worse, but simply one to be judged on the basis of his merits and in accord with the content of his character. Not only does the white liberal think this in his own head—he expects other people to think in these terms as well and notes it as an exception when he finds a situation in which he isn't treated according to his own idea of how a person ought to be treated. No wonder then that it comes as such a great shock for the white liberal to discover that no matter how hard he tries, he does not fit in with the rich, simply because, in fact, he is not rich. He is not welcome among the rich for the simple reason that, in the long run, he can't afford the membership dues. It's nothing personal, he is told in a hushed tone by a luxury store clerk (probably a fellow white liberal) informing him that his credit card has been declined. The strength of his ideology is such that it takes awhile for this lesson to set in, but reality has a funny way of asserting itself repeatedly despite our protestations.

After enough of these melancholy vacations, and after throwing away significant amounts of perfectly good money that could've actually been used to purchase the goods and services that he needs in order to live, the white liberal gets the message. Over time and through experience, he discovers that he is not welcome among the rich, and as such, he no longer feels welcome even vacationing in their establishments. Unused to this feeling of apartness, or unused to seeing his apartness confirmed so objectively, the white liberal cultivates a certain resentment. Interestingly, the resentment of the rich is more characteristic of the white liberal than it is of the dark working class. Unable to pass, unable to afford even such temporary vacations, the members of the dark working class never suppose that the gulf that separates them from the rich is one that could be bridged. Accordingly, their unwelcomeness among the rich is taken as a fact of life rather than as a provocation for an emotion so acutely personal as resentment.

What does the white liberal's resentment look like concretely? He stops looking for the progressively smaller living spaces that he can afford in the scarce "good" urban neighborhoods and instead moves to slightly less "good" urban neighborhoods (which means living in closer proximity to the dark working class) or even, gasp, to the suburbs (where at least he can be alone, although there is always the perpetual threat that rednecks and the dark working class are encroaching). The white liberal cannot actually move to the country because he has never learned the sorts of self-reliant skills that country life requires and, ultimately, even if he could acquire these skills, he cannot tolerate his own company. He quits the expensive habit of drinking wine and instead cultivates a taste for bitter and hoppy microbrews and sweet vinegar-like Belgian beers. He stops shopping in department stores and instead finds his clothes at big box stores and, even, thrift stores. He stops going out to overpriced trendy restaurants and instead sticks to hamburgers and pizza, or cheap ethnic food, and if things get really bad, he even starts to cook for himself. He stops going to the theater and instead stays home and watches movies that he downloads from the internet.

Resentment of the fact that he is not rich leads the white liberal to cultivate any number of unique and eccentric cultural tastes—the hipster transvaluation of redneck culture is but one particularly striking example. Does the white liberal ever realize that he does all of this and so much more—SWPL is a great compendium of these things—out of resentment for the rich? No, he does not. His resentment is a trauma which cannot be spoken, but precisely for that reason, it is one which he continuously rehearses.

What would it mean to speak this resentment, to give it the name that it deserves? For white liberals, it would mean to recognize that the nature of their predicament (and the more severe predicament of the dark working class as well) stems most essentially from the fact that rich people exist. It is not enough to maintain an attitude of polite resignation with respect to the rich; nor is it feasible to attempt to ignore them or to pretend that they are irrelevant. The fact is that while there are not very many of them, rich people exert an inordinate influence upon our culture, our values, our beliefs, our social interactions, and perhaps most importantly, our material survival.

As far as the rich are concerned, the attitude cannot any longer be the one of "live and let live" that white liberals, in their harmlessness and denial, have sought to maintain. The rich simply cannot be allowed to continue getting away with paying tax at the absurdly low capital gains rate of 15% while all the rest of us see our incomes dwindle and our social services cut. So many of us today, even white liberals, enjoy fewer and fewer of the routine privileges that are supposed to go along with being a citizen of an industrialized country. Today, even many white liberals find themselves with no real income, no way to afford seeing a doctor or a dentist without filing for bankruptcy, no efficient way to get from place to place, and no affordable place to live. If any of this is to change for white liberals, they must drastically change their attitude of "live and let live" toward the rich. A rich man who lives means many a poor man who does not. It really is that simple. "Kill or be killed" has always been and continues to be a more accurate statement regarding the relationship between the classes. It is time that white liberals awaken to this reality.

2.2   *The Social Limbo of White Liberals*

Socially, white liberals live lives of quiet desperation in isolation from: the elite (due to: insufficient funds), rednecks (due to: lack of physical proximity and the reluctance to overcome an often extreme mismatch of cultural values), and the darker races (due to: an acquired timidity in response to real and/or perceived difference, the reluctance to overcome an often extreme mismatch of cultural values, and fear of associating too closely with those on the business end of white supremacy with respect to exploitative labor, police violence, civic violence, etc.). White liberals, like all species, often desire to be around their own kind. The trouble being that they do not really have a socially distinct existence—i.e., they depend upon the poor for their essential material resources and the governmental and corporate institutions dominated by the interests of the rich for their provisional exemption from the more exploitative forms of labor—and so this instinctual desire for similarity and commonality often leads to literal aloneness.

Or, white liberals' condition of material and cultural dependence would lead to their aloneness, *except for the fact that they cluster together in urban areas.* The city is the only environment sufficiently dense as to sustain a significant number of white liberals within close physical proximity to one another. This is why white liberals love *New York City* so much (as SWPL attests). Their position of material, social, and cultural limbo makes it incredibly difficult for white liberals to associate with members of other groups (e.g., rednecks, the dark working class, the elite). Accordingly, urban environs which can sustain a large number of white liberals often provide the only meaningful possibilities for them to engage in significant amounts of social behavior.

Of course, the presence of a significant number of white liberals within a limited geographic area can always and only mean one thing: there is an even larger dark working class nearby. Without the dark working class supplying their material necessities, white liberals simply could not exist. However, while they can never be too far from a significant dark working class population, still white liberals do their best to isolate themselves into neighborhoods in which they are "safe" from the dark working class. Accordingly, most interactions between white liberals and the dark working class take place primarily in the carefully constrained context of the latter providing a service of some sort to the former (e.g., food, childcare, etc.).

What keeps white liberals from living the values they espouse and actually associating with the dark working class? At every stage of life, white liberals are socially and economically discouraged from associating too closely with the dark working class. Living in dark working class neighborhoods means agreeing to: higher insurance payments, diminished access to "public" services (e.g., timely police and fire department response, well-maintained roadways, functional public transportation, well-funded schools, etc.), and fewer adjacent employment opportunities (especially at a living wage). If given a choice, who would opt for such a fate? As opposed to the dark working class, white liberals are indeed given this choice. Accordingly, while white liberals may believe in the equality of the dark working class in the abstract, rarely do they actually live with them when they can afford not to.

Nor are white liberals really welcome to engage in any meaningful level of social association with the rich. The social and physical divisions between the rich and white liberals are often nearly as extreme as those between white liberals and the poor. Thanks to his complexion, a white liberal may indeed be free to walk down the street in the Upper East Side without being hassled by the cops (though in suburban elite neighborhoods, like those of the Los Angeles area, anyone of any complexion who is walking anywhere at night, rather than driving, is inherently suspect). However, this welcome extends only so far—a white liberal could no more afford to go out to dinner on a regular basis in an elite neighborhood than he could afford to live there. In the short term, a white liberal may indeed be able to pass for elite, but only by putting oneself into hock simply for the sake of experiencing a limited and brief belonging with those of true material comfort, i.e., those unlike oneself. In the end, however, such a temporary and fleeting vacation from reality—e.g., the birthday dinner at a 5 Star restaurant, the summer sublet in a neighborhood one could never otherwise afford—only serves to underscore the very fact of the white liberal's fundamental apartness from such environs.

Unwelcome among the rich, and unwelcoming to the idea of keeping too close company with the dark working class, white liberals cluster in their own urban neighborhoods or in suburban college towns. The experience of being unable to fit within the properly elite institutions of the rich is deeply frustrating for white liberals, who after all, are used to assuming that their white skin allows them to go wherever they want. However, the white liberal compensates for his own exclusion from the rich by fleeing to his own institutions, establishments, and geographic spaces (e.g., neighborhoods, suburbs, etc.)

that more or less intentionally exclude the dark working class.

At least white liberals are allowed to vacation more or less freely among the elite when they can afford it. Generally speaking, white liberals do not extend an invitation to the dark working class to partake in their institutions and neighborhoods, even when the latter come equipped with their own hard-earned money. The very presence of members of the dark working class in white liberal enclaves is often in and of itself enough to motivate considerable suspicion and/or resentment, if not outright harassment and even violence on the part of police and/or corporate enforcers (e.g., security guards). In some intensely ideological liberal areas, it is more or less acceptable to be dark. In others, it is more or less all right to be working class. Almost nowhere is it possible to be both dark and working class without incurring suspicion and/or danger.

This exclusivity of white liberal areas with respect to the dark working class should not come as a great surprise even though it is contradicted by the white liberal's stated ideology of equality; this exclusivity stems from the difference in material conditions between the two groups and, thus, it goes deeper than ideology. The most essential characteristic of the American dream is not that of having what others have—it's having what someone else is denied. As long as there's one person left poorer than you, the Dream still lives! Even the dark working class often clings to their own version of the American Dream, instituting and enforcing strict racial, cultural, and social hierarchies amongst themselves.

The desirability of a given physical location as a habitat for a cluster of white liberals can easily be assessed with respect to only a couple of factors: 1, there need be a relatively close (but not overly close) contingent of the dark working class whose cheap labor can be relied upon to keep consumer prices low enough for white liberals to afford the goods and services which they enjoy and; 2, there need be at least a handful of elite-endowed cultural and economic institutions nearby. In economic terms, white liberals require the following elite-driven institutions within their habitat (e.g., as sites of employment): banks, courts, universities, hospitals, professional practices, intellectual property and/or financial management companies, endowed non-profit organizations, etc. In cultural terms, white liberals rely upon the presence of the following elite-driven institutions: museums, art galleries, concert halls, theaters, universities, media outlets, etc. White liberals buy their (temporary, contingent, fleeting, elusive, vanishing) freedom from poverty with the dispensations they receive from the rich; the poor provide them what they need to live and the rich tell them who they are.

2.2.1. *White Liberal Education as* Bildungsroman

Almost everything white liberals do as social, economic, and cultural actors is in some way marked by their relationship to the educational system. Throughout life, education provides the constant backdrop—the one unerring key—for white liberals to turn to in understanding their endeavors and the world around them. Early in life, white liberal parents teach their children to value the value of education— "school is your work" these parents often tell their children as a means of motivation. Unsurprisingly, the white liberal coming-of-age story almost invariably follows the same pattern. For the young white liberal, the measure of attaining an identity—the mark of an autonomous selfhood—consists in the degree to which the value of education migrates from an external demand (insisted upon by parents, teachers, and other authority figures) to a properly internalized commitment. The young white liberal becomes such insofar as he or she sees the value of education as occupying a central place in who it is that he or she endeavors to become; adhering to this narrative progression constitutes the sole hope of white liberal becoming. For the young white liberal to deviate from the *Bildungsroman* of faith in education—self-instilled belief manifested by self-directed purposive action towards advancement in the educational system for the sake of meaning and salvation—is to risk turning one's life into an unintelligible picaresque. Education constitutes the true white liberal religion and it is adhered to with just as much (if not more) fervor and devotion among supposed atheists.

Recognizing the deeply religious power with which many in our society (and white liberals in particular) endow the educational system is essential for making sense of the otherwise unfathomable amounts of time, money, and effort that many parents expend in order to assure that *their* children will be the ones to reap the benefits of the educational system. Taken to the heights of absurdity, the attempt to advance one's own child ahead of others on the educational track begins in earnest—at least for a select group of particularly obsessive upper middle class parents—with the attempt to secure a position in an expensive private preschool. This commitment continues with nearly unabated tenacity until the day that the child secures admission to an Ivy League university. Of course, some parents don't stop even then, continuing to help their children with homework and networking throughout college and on into graduate school and/or professional employment. This phenomenon of "helicopter parenting" as it has come to be known needs to be seen for what it is: a sign of desperation. More specifically, helicopter parenting shows the depth and prevalence of the fear among middle class parents that, without their constant vigilance, their children will fall into the working class.

One of the interesting things to note about the phenomenon of helicopter parenting is that the nature of the objective depends upon much more than ensuring your child's success in formal educational institutions alone. Today, formal academic preparation is simply not enough to procure the socioeconomic advantages of an elite education for your child. For many elite universities today, academic performance is a generally necessary but by itself insufficient condition for securing admission. [11] These universities want their students to be "well-rounded" people who pursue "extra-curricular interests" in things like athletics, politics, community service, music, literature, and art (so long as these interests exhibit properly bourgeois sensibilities). While school may indeed be akin to work for the children of the middle class, elite universities (and preschools) also believe that "all work and no play makes Jack a dull boy." However, rather than reducing the environment of competition surrounding entrance to elite academic institutions, the broadening of admissions criteria has only resulted in expanding the competition for these spots to encompass nearly every aspect of a child's life. Accordingly, the successful helicopter parent has to go much further than merely directing his or her child's academic preparation and academically relevant

---

[11] There was a time, early in the 20th Century, when Ivy League universities relied solely upon academic performance as a basis for admission. However, a significant problem arose due to this approach to admissions. Put simply, too many Jews were being let in. The contemporary collegiate admissions process (the personal essay, the personal interview, the importance placed upon athletics, etc.) arose directly as a corrective measure to this Jewish problem (i.e., the fact that Jews were simply academically outperforming their WASP counterparts). See: Jerome Karabel, *The Chosen: The Hidden History of Admission and Exclusion at Harvard, Yale, and Princeton* (New York: Mariner Books, 2006).

activities. Every hour of the day, and every aspect of life, need be measured for its utility (or lack thereof) in contributing to a child's admissions portfolio.

There is much about the phenomenon of helicopter parenting which attests to the absurdity of our society's educational system, as well as our society's values and priorities generally speaking. However, for our present purposes—i.e., examining the conditions of existence which inform the lives of the white liberal species, education being the most central among said conditions—helicopter parenting is most interesting as a limit case or a mostly negative example. The preoccupation with the potential socioeconomic advantages of elite education upon which helicopter parenting derives is clearly a white liberal obsession. However, despite their actions being motivated by a similar paranoia, there is a great difference between the philosophy of education manifested by helicopter parents and the philosophy of education that is proper to the true white liberal.

Helicopter parents pursue their paranoid obsession with their children's education for different reasons and through different methods than the devotional practices which characterize the properly white liberal faith in education. Taken to its most brutal and totalizing extreme, helicopter parenting regards education (and hence pre-adult life as a whole) as a purely instrumental objective for the procurement of socioeconomic advantages. For the true helicopter parent, results are all that matters. From this vantage, admission defines the parameters for an essentially zero-sum game: either your child gets in (to the right school, with the right scholarship package, etc.) or she doesn't.

By contrast, the measure of white liberal coming-of-age is not simply educational achievement alone. The goal of white liberal parenting is to instill their young with an internally directed devotion to the faith of education, apart from the specific facts of educational achievement. When education is conceived as the ground for an absolute system of faith, as it is for white liberals, its value is regarded as something more and something other than the incidental socioeconomic advantages that may or may not result from its pursuit.

The true white liberal views the quest for education as a *process*. Getting into the right school is a nice result, to be sure. But, what is of primary importance for the true white liberal is not the achievement of a winning result, but rather how the serious game of education is played. To play the game of education in the right way means playing according to the right rules (i.e., fairly), for the right stakes (i.e., the game itself), and with the right motivation (i.e., as an expression of internally-generated goals rather than as a competition for externally-defined rewards). The point is not simply to get one's child into the right school so that he or she will have a comfortable and/or productive life. Rather, the goal is to spur one's child to pursue education as a value unto itself and to embrace its pursuit as more than a rote and empty ritual.

The white liberal educational ideal consists in a process which is both self-generated and self-generating. What's being decided in the course of education is the very nature of a child's soul; as such, it is ultimately the soul itself which will have to provide the process with its true and proper direction. Accordingly, the proper role of the parent in such an educational process consists not in that of the demanding task master, but rather that of the patient and prudent facilitator. Given these fundamental differences among the two groups with respect to how they view the purpose and meaning of education, not to mention the means by which education ought to be pursued, it is unsurprising that white liberals are often among the most harshly critical of helicopter parenting.[12]

Of course, in actual practice, the contrast between these two educational philosophies will be less clear than we have made it here for illustrational purposes. Generally speaking, parents rely upon some mixture between the two philosophies, not to mention the much simpler approach suggested by inattention and neglect (benign and otherwise). Helicopter parenting still relies upon activating a child's self-motivation to some degree. In fact, many helicopter parents view themselves as mere facilitators—surrounding their children 24 hours a day with activities and lessons devoted to things in which their children express some sort of initial interest. Similarly, while the white

---

[12] See: Joan Acocella, "The Child Trap: The Rise of Overparenting," *New Yorker*, November 17 2008.

liberal educational ideal is that of a child directing the course of his or her own educational process, in absolute terms this is of course a complete fiction. The particular mixture adopted from among these contrasting styles will of course depend upon the whole range of cultural and socioeconomic complexities relevant to the parents' and children's immediate context.

Despite what the most devout white liberal parents tell themselves, a child's love for learning (especially for those limited subjects which count for social rewards) still has to be cultivated in one manner or another. The art of white liberal parenting consists in spurring one's child to develop just such a cultivated taste in academic subjects while encouraging the child to believe that it was he or she who desired such tastes in the first place. And, of course, white liberals are often starkly aware of (if not deeply paranoid about) the real consequences that result from a child's failure to outperform his or her peers academically. Just as whiteness comes in contrasting polarities which despite their differences are still expressive of the same underlying social facts, the same is true for middle class philosophies of education.

2.3   The Economic Limbo of White Liberals

Economically, white liberals find themselves in a state of limbo primarily in the following respect: they are relatively insulated from the most exploitative forms of labor but, unlike the rich, rarely do they profit from that labor directly other than in their capacity as consumers. This insulation from the fate of the dark working class exists for white liberals largely as a special dispensation which they receive courtesy of the rich. Practically, this dispensation takes the form of *creditability*—i.e., what Frank Fukuyama has simply called "trust."[13] White liberals are what they are insofar as they have access to things like loans (business, consumer, student, etc.), education, and desk jobs. All of the institutions which extend these sorts of credit are owned, bought, and paid for by the rich. Accordingly, when the rich extend credit to white liberals far in excess to what they extend to the dark working class it is because they feel that white liberals will not betray their *trust*. In what does this trust consist? In many large things, and many small things but most of all in the understanding that the rich are the ones who get to decide who is trustworthy and who is not.

White liberals are saved from the economic fate of the dark working class (and that of many rednecks as well) thanks to: entrenched inequalities in educational funding that ensure greater opportunities for children born into families and communities of higher socio-economic status and lighter skin, a criminal justice system that routinely overlooks the indiscretions of middle class white youth while severely (and often preemptively) punishing the (real or perceived) indiscretions of poor and/or dark youth, the special dispensation that the business community grants to

---

[13] Francis Fukuyama, *Trust: The Social Virtues and the Creation of Prosperity* (New York: Free Press, 1995).

the white middle class by providing them with access to quality jobs, loans, and real estate (far in excess to the access offered to any other group of similar financial status). However, the nature of the institutional advantages provided to white liberals—which, above all else, ensure their exemption from more exploitative forms of labor—is such that they are rarely if ever given out right. Rather, these advantages are given (1) on the basis of prior successful performances of white privilege and/or (2) under the threat of being revoked at any time, should white liberals fail at successfully performing their privilege.

The stakes of white privilege are clearly demonstrable with respect to what happens to white liberals if and when they act in a manner which violates the trust instilled in them by the rich. Should white liberals ever act in a way which tarnishes the image of whiteness as a property of respectable, responsible, affluent, hard-working, law-abiding consumers, they may very well find themselves marked untrustworthy. Accordingly, white liberals must constantly monitor their credit score (in our society, even having *no* debt comes with drastic consequences), their health insurance status (getting sick while uninsured is the single largest cause of bankruptcy), their children's educational progress (most importantly, their test scores), and their own (and their children's) psychopharmaceutical state (while drug use constitutes one of the few possible ways to tolerate the monotony of a desk job, many of these jobs now require routine drug testing; similarly, getting convicted of a drug offense means losing one's eligibility to receive federal student aid).

Keep in mind that while the initial punishment for any one of these offenses may by itself seem relatively minor, white privilege functions as a constellation of overlapping opportunities and responsibilities. Revocation or abdication of any single opportunity or responsibility may in turn result in drastically fewer opportunities and responsibilities even with respect to domains of privilege that seem at first to be entirely unrelated. For example, your children's chances for future success are enhanced by living in the "right" neighborhood; living in the "right" neighborhood requires good credit; this in turn generally requires a steady, well-paying job; in our post-industrial society, such jobs generally require education (generally speaking, the more prestigious and expensive the education, the better the job). Who would even think at the time of receiving a drug conviction as a young adult (and thereby becoming ineligible for federal student aid) that you were lowering not only your own, but also your children's opportunities of educational success? In practice, and statistically over the long run, this is precisely what such a conviction means.

Now, depending upon their means, a given white person may have the socioeconomic resources to fight a drug charge or any other equally dangerous threat to their white privilege that may arise at a given moment. And, naturally, white folk are much more likely than black or brown folk to have access to the socioeconomic resources necessary for such petitions (e.g., lawyers that are competent, diligent, and well-respected, i.e., by white people). However, whiteness in and of itself is not any kind of guarantee—and the fact that white privilege is constantly under threat is precisely what requires its perpetual performance. The fact of the matter is: white liberals have to work (and how!) in order to stay white. No wonder a compendium like SWPL has sprung up in order to remind them of all that they must do!

In addition to the immense disparities of wealth evident between the two groups, this is one of the clearest differences between white liberals and the elite. For white liberals, life comes with few opportunities for second acts. Commit a sin early in life (e.g., a petty crime, dropping out of school, failing to pay your debts) and watch how fast your exemption from the most exploitative labor flees; see just how hard it is to earn back the trust of rich white people and their representatives (not to say that it is ever strictly impossible—if it was impossible, this would encourage those on the lower end of the trust scale to simply give up at being white, which the rich would never want them to do). For the elite, on the other hand, there are seemingly infinite opportunities. A member of the elite can: be of sub-average intelligence, do poorly at school, fail completely in business life, be a habitual alcoholic, have a well-documented history of cocaine use, and still become President of the United States of America if he so chooses (i.e., if he is not qualified for any other more lucrative and distinguished position).

The trust afforded to white liberals is only one side of the economic equation in which they exist. In order to sustain an economy—regional and global—capable of supporting a small number of white liberals, there must always be a much, much larger dark working class. Globally, white liberals depend upon the dark working class for the following modes of labor: growing their coffee, tea, and other inebriants, picking their food, sewing their clothes, manufacturing their computers and gadgets, wresting raw materials from the earth, etc. Regionally, white liberals depend upon the dark working class for the following modes of labor: cooking their food, doing their dishes, stocking their shelves, fixing their cars, cleaning up their messes, watching their kids, building their homes, etc. In a more equitable world economy, complexion and nationality would not play a role—much less the enormous one which these factors play today—in determining who does what for whom. If such a change ever took place on a global level, it would in turn implicate similarly drastic changes for the division of labor within any and all of the world's regions. Namely, it would mean that white people would have to relearn how to support themselves materially in all of the various ways which they have forgotten today.

Money is the strongest glue by which whiteness sticks. The economic limbo of white liberals proceeds through the dogged attempt to make their whiteness stick with earned trust rather than money. However, of these two bonds, trust is by far the less enduring; unlike money, trust can always be revoked. In trying so hard to earn the trust of the elite, white liberals thereby alienate themselves from the dark working class. Unfortunately, white liberals fail to see this alienation until after the fact; once they try to remedy their alienation with sentiment or charity, it is already too late; by then, they are already who and what they are—a creature without the means to affect the fundamental terms of its existence.

2.3.1 The Limits of a Liberal Education

In a sense, we can admire white liberals for their attempt to instill in their children a love of learning that transcends the material advantages that may or may not accompany education. If this view at least suggests a realistic acknowledgement of the fact that in no way does education in and of itself guarantee particular socioeconomic advantages, this realism is itself the mark of a deeper naiveté. Namely, white liberals assume that the world is structured in such a way that even though education offers no material guarantees, their children need little if anything else in order to survive. So devout are white liberals in their faith in education that they never bother to examine whether or not it is reasonable to think that education alone can guarantee their children's survival. Moreover, even if the white liberal's faith in education is indeed reasonable in the sense that recent history has shown its utility as an adaptive mechanism for the survival of the species, there is still reason to be critical.

For one thing, there will come a day—and the attentive observer has much reason to think that such a day may not be very far off—when this mechanism will no longer work. The central problem with such an article of faith is not its content but the very fact that it is held as a dogma which is passed down, recited, and practiced without its adherents pausing to consider how and why it works if and when it does so. That is, at present white liberals are resolutely unwilling to ask the question: what other material conditions are necessary in order for the faith in education to procure material survival for its adherents? There is a clear advantage to preserving this miraculous—and indeed *deus ex machina*—view of the benefits of education: such a faith allows white liberals to go on living without having to consider upon what or whom their livelihood depends.

The drawbacks of relying upon education to work without seeking an explanation for how it works are primarily two-fold: 1, the adherents cannot decide for themselves and on the margins if their faith is really in their own long-term interests and 2, apart from their own prospective gains and losses, the adherents cannot see how their faith affects the circumstances of others, the dark working class and poor rednecks in particular. In the process of devoting their time and effort to the pursuit of education to the enormous extent that they do, white liberals progressively lose their ability to contribute to other sectors of the labor market. As such, their material position becomes tied to the educational system to an almost unthinkable degree. Recognizing this predicament, white liberals correctly see that their success (as beneficiaries of the educational system) depends upon the continued growth of the educational system as a whole.

There is one essential problem for the white liberal ideal of education for everyone: the more accessible education becomes, the fewer are its material advantages. There is a definite limit concerning the number of people who can enjoy the socioeconomic advantages reaped through the educational system at any one time. As has become demonstrably clear in recent years, increasing the availability of higher education dilutes the finite socioeconomic advantages that come from higher education: the more college degrees there are the less they count for. While there may be more and more of us living on Earth every day, at any given time there is a finite limit to how many people can survive without procuring their own material resources.

The skyrocketing percentage of the population attending higher education in post-industrial societies over the past 50 years has directly coincided with the move of manufacturing to the global South. What this means is: those desk jobs that were, for but a brief amount of time, considered the god-given privilege of any college graduate had to come from somewhere. For there to be money in the pushing around of paper and/or magnetically-encoded information requires that such paper and information correspond to some real change in physical material undertaken by someone somewhere. The desk jobs in post-industrial societies do not create themselves; those "jobs" are created by compelling the dark working class around the world to enter into the most exploitative forms of labor: mining and manufacturing. Extending education to greater numbers does nothing to change this fact. Putting your children in higher education means that someone else's children, tomorrow if not today, will be thrown into the mines and sweatshops.

If this is indeed the case—and I would assert that considered for the world as a whole and over the long-run indeed it is—how have white liberals managed to convince themselves that education is in the benefit of everyone? Because, having more or less cornered the educational labor market, the more people who enter into education and the more education they pursue, the more white liberals benefit. In other words, extending education to wider swathes of the population probably does little or nothing to benefit the world population as a whole, but it does clearly and directly benefit white liberals. White liberals adopt their chosen ideology for the same reason that ideologies are adopted generally: for the sake of *immediate* material preservation (at the cost of *continued* material preservation).

However, by relying upon education as their survival strategy, white liberals effectively alienate themselves from the dark working class and thus ultimately from themselves as well. By preaching the faith of education as the path to salvation, white liberals perpetuate the myth that the world can continue to exist without anyone having to do real work—i.e., mining, manufacturing, and agriculture. In the long run, it is not white liberals who benefit from this myth; rather, it is the elite, who use the fantasy that someday—in the always deferred future—no one will have to work as a means of excusing the depraved working conditions encountered in the more exploitative forms of labor.

This fantasy—that in the future, on the day when our productive technologies reach their culmination, back-breaking labor will no longer be necessary—provides a means of convincing white liberals to accept their unique place in the exploitation of the dark working class. If the dark working class is exploited, then it is only for their own good, at least in the (perpetually deferred) future, white liberals tell themselves when and if the problem ever occurs to them. The more that white liberals believe this lie, the easier it is for them to accept their own place of relative privilege. This position of privilege—that is to say, the entirety of what makes white liberal existence possible—comes from the dispensation provided to white liberals by the rich. This dispensation is provided to white liberals in exchange for their service in perpetuating and exacerbating the exploitation of the dark working class. Preaching the absolute faith of education is not only how white liberals keep themselves going; it's also how they pay their dues to the rich—i.e., by enslaving the poor.

In all this, white liberals never stop to ask: what is the logical end-point of our complete and unerring faith in education? Even the most cursory reflection on the matter would show that such an end-point could never be achieved in fact—i.e., having every man, woman, and child on the planet employed in either educating or being educated is patently absurd as it leaves no one left to gather food. However, there are many reasons for believing in the impossible; there is no such thing as a fantasy that is sold without someone reaping its profits. When white liberals advocate for their faith in education, they are indeed the ones who benefit at least in the short-term. And, as always, it is the rich who are the ones that benefit in the end.

Having already secured the benefits of the educational system for themselves—thanks to the advantages they've received from the history of white supremacist efforts to keep the dark working class on the bottom of the wage scale—white liberals can safely and confidently advocate for the extension of educational opportunities to the dark working class as a direct extension of their own economic interests. As this ideology works in practice, members of the dark working class enter the educational system (often at ridiculously expensive for-profit colleges staffed by desperate white liberals who can find no other employment with their education[14]) and this in turn

---

[14] As Ivory A. Toldson reports: "The top 10 colleges for enrolling black males consist of three for-profit colleges, four community colleges and three public four-year institutions.

creates opportunities for already well-educated white liberals to subsist by educating them. In this manner, white liberals collaborate with the elite in the process of extracting the wages paid to the dark working class.

The for-profit model of higher education has matured greatly over the past 15 years. Immense profits also continue to be made by the private educational material corporations that serve "public schools." Cumulatively, the educational system provides an additional means of depriving the working class in general, and the dark working class in particular, of a portion of their wages—through taxes, bonds, lottery schemes, tuition, and fees—and putting that money back where it belongs: in the hands of the elite.

Why does it benefit elites when the working class has less money? Isn't this money that could go to consumer spending, and thus, their own coffers? Depriving the working class of money keeps them desperate and this, in turn, benefits the rich immensely. Various usury practices—check cashing fees, payday advances, predatory loans, etc.— essentially turn the working class into indentured servants. Keeping the working class in a position of perpetual desperation ensures that they will continue

---

The University of Phoenix online campus reported 847 black male students in 2001 and 21,802 in 2011, making it the nation's top enroller of black male students. Second is Ashford University, which reported 23 black males in 2001 and 15,081 in 2011." http://www.theroot.com/views/more-black-men-jail-college-wrong

to work for lower wages and in more physically dangerous circumstances than they would otherwise.

It is deeply myopic to assume that simply because the money that the working class contributes to educational institutions does not go to the elite directly that this means that the money doesn't end up in the hands of the elite in the end. When the working class gives its hard-earned money to educational institutions, they are largely giving it to white liberals. In turn, white liberals (thanks to their student loan debts, expensive elite-derived tastes, fear of living in cheaper working class neighborhoods, and the fact that they have no real knowledge of how to turn money into productive capital) can be trusted to give their money back to the elites. In other words, the rich don't really lose the money that the dark working class contributes to the educational mechanism—the money just has to pass all too briefly through the hands of white liberals on its way to returning to them. If white liberals can survive on education alone, it is because education itself performs a function which the rich find valuable: namely, depriving workers' of their wages and, just as importantly, their class consciousness. This is the stuff dreams are made of.

2.4   *What's the Matter with San Francisco?: How White Liberals Benefit from Conservative Politics (in the Short-Run)*

It may seem queer that we have not as of yet overtly discussed the matter of the white liberal's political orientation. This is not an accident. Political orientation is a matter that is best understood in relation to the facts of life out of which it grows. While the name "white liberal" suggests that politics plays a primary role in defining the nature of the species in question, we have instead sought to focus first and foremost upon the facts of life relevant to this species. Now, at last, we will examine the connection between the white liberal's political orientation and the limbic facts of life that define his material, social, and cultural existence.

Having sketched the white liberal as a creature of limbo, we are once again struck by the peculiar fact that such a creature exists, even as an idea. In terms of economic theory, there is no essential reason that white liberals need to exist; so much of the world, and many economies, get along without them. To put it in other terms: what keeps white liberals from wholly siding with the elite? Sure, there is the fact that they don't have enough money. But look at all the things that white liberals have to thank the elite for: nearly the entirety of their "culture" (indeed, white liberals' cultural preferences tend to be based in either or both: a consumerist form of elite values or a resentful reaction to their indoctrination in elite values), protection under the law, and freedom from the worst kinds of labor. Why are white liberals so ungrateful? Why, even if it's only just pretending, do they ever side with the dark and/or the poor politically? Wouldn't capitalism be so much simpler if we were all Republicans?

In short, I want to turn the famous question that Thomas Frank asked before the 2004 election on its head.[15] From my point of view, we should not be asking: What's the matter with Kansas? The real mystery is: What's the matter with San Francisco? Immediate incentives are always there to side with the elite—after all, they're the people with all of the money, and therefore, all of the influence. Why should this fact surprise us? Frank's claim was that there are a substantial number of poor white people (i.e., rednecks) who vote to provide the elite with more money and who thus take money away from themselves in the process because they're voting with cultural rather than economic interests in mind. I submit that a more thorough-going analysis of the matter reveals that rednecks do indeed vote for the party of the elite out of concern for their own economic interests.[16] Besides the obvious cultural issues that are involved, which Frank does indeed address, rednecks vote for Republicans because doing

---

[15] Thomas Frank, *What's the Matter with Kansas?: How Conservatives Won the Heart of America* (New York: Metropolitan Books, 2004).

[16] The following analysis of the manner in which voting for conservative candidates is actually in rednecks' own economic interests has the ability to explain the fact that, contrary to Dr. Frank's explanation, the vast majority of rednecks of all income brackets indicate economics (rather than cultural issues) as the most important issue when deciding who to vote for. For a criticism of various aspects of Frank's Kansas thesis supported by empirical data see: Larry M. Bartels, "What's the Matter with *What's the Matter with Kansas?*," *Quarterly Journal of Political Science*, no. 1 (2006).

so *takes money away* from the darker races, thus insuring that the darker races stay at the bottom of the wage ladder.

The agreement between elites and rednecks is perfectly straight-forward and, I would allege, in the short-term economic interests of both parties: vote for our party, the elites say, and we'll take money away from social services. Sure, we know that you rednecks could get money from those social services but so could black and brown people. If you let us take the money away from social services, we'll make sure to use that money privately to fund the kinds of churches and other civic institutions that we know primarily rural white people go to and publicly to create jobs in industries (e.g., defense, corrections, etc.) based in rural and exurban areas (where fewer black and brown people live). Moreover, we'll do our best to get rid of environmental regulations in order to support jobs in rural redneck-staffed industries that do the dirty, polluting work that the rest of society wants to benefit from but not see. In short, we both get more money by making sure black and brown folk don't get any!

Now, in the long-term, when their beloved pensions suddenly start to burst at the seams and when social services are cut due to manufactured local and state budget crises, rednecks are indeed getting hoodwinked by supporting Republicans. However, in the short-term, the benefits of depriving others of resources are often nearly as tangible as the benefits of getting resources for oneself: lower wages for the working class as a whole keeps the prices of many goods and services low. Also, free trade policies mean that the working class in this country benefits from the exploitation of the working class of the rest of the world. The only way that these sorts of consumer benefits—that come from the exploitation of the working class as a whole, both domestically and abroad—actually amount to a net gain is if, somehow, the deflation of consumer prices is not accompanied by a similar deflation in wages for whites.

Clearly, this economic situation of falling (or stagnating) prices of goods and services and stagnating (or rising) wages cannot continue indefinitely for the working class as a whole, given that a gain in one column comes directly from a loss in the other. However, if for some economically inexplicable reason, a particularly privileged portion of the working class sees their wages remain constant while wages fall for the working class as a whole, then that privileged portion of the working class will indeed benefit (in the short-term, as consumers) from the exploitation of their own class. Indeed, members of this privileged portion of the working class may even see their wages fall, but still assess the exploitation of their class as a net gain, as long as over that same period, wages fall more dramatically for the rest of the working class.

When rednecks vote Republican, this is what they are voting for: to be a member of the (only comparatively) privileged part of the working class that benefits from the enslavement of the working class as a whole. What possible method could there be for dividing the working class amongst itself, so that a small portion of the total group will benefit from the exploitation of the group as a whole? Why race, gender, and citizenship status are time-honored for their effectiveness in doing just that! This is precisely the calculus which drives white men across income brackets to vote Republican disproportionately to all other demographic groups. Rednecks may at times be miscalculating their economic interests when they vote for Republicans, and in the long-term they certainly are, but that doesn't mean that the calculation is so one-sided or obvious as it might at first appear. Indeed, many rednecks, even quite poor ones, are likely correct when they discern that it is in their individual short-term interests to vote Republican. *White supremacy is an economic interest and not just for the rich.*

So what's wrong with white liberals? Why do they fail to see what their less educated redneck brethren do? Namely, that if you're white, white supremacist policies which hurt the working class as a whole may still help *you*. Why do white liberals, and white liberal men in particular, continue to reject policies and candidates that would actually most benefit their immediate economic interests? This is a particularly mysterious phenomenon when we recall that in some respects, white liberals are even better situated to benefit from white supremacist economics than rednecks. White liberals, after all, often receive an education which thoroughly inculcates them with elite cultural values. As such, it would seem that they are natural allies to the elite. And yet, for some economically inexplicable reason, rather than making whites align with the elite as one would suppose, education often seems to have the opposite effect.

The point is this: it pays (often handsomely) to keep the dark working class in their place (at least for select individuals and/or groups and over the short-term). If white liberals oppose elite interests at all—or simply support those interests less enthusiastically than they otherwise could (e.g., by voting Republican)—then even this modest measure of resistance is still somewhat remarkable. This leads us to ask, why do they do it? That is to say, what social factors make it possible for white liberals to resist elite interests politically, however minimal their resistance to those interests might be? As we shall see, the short answer to this question involves the place that white liberals serve in the social function of education. However, explaining why and how their role in education allows white liberals to be liberal and to still benefit from white supremacy at the same time is a difficult matter.

First, let us begin from the assumption that there is some way in which white liberals' chosen ideology allows them to survive materially—or that, at the very least, such an ideology is not directly contrary to their survival in the short-term. One possible explanation for the fact that white liberals are able to survive—and moreover, to procure for themselves an exemption from the more exploitative forms of labor—while still having an ideology which is contrary to the interests of the elite (at least in theory) is that there are ways in which white liberals benefit from elite-supported white supremacist politics without needing to endorse that ideology explicitly. For one thing, the fact that rednecks often support policies that divide the working class along white supremacist lines often means that where these policies succeed, white liberals benefit regardless of whether they themselves actually support the policies directly. From this vantage, the politics of white liberals can be regarded as a kind of "triangulation" strategy. White liberals can support their own liberal policies and candidates (in the effort to keep their wages and benefits from falling drastically) while at the same time benefitting from the conservative policies and candidates that attempt to hurt the working class as a whole, but skew towards hurting the dark working class more than others.

While it may be contrary to their stated ideology of equality, white liberals benefit directly from the fact that so many black and brown folk are behind bars. So too do they benefit directly from an educational system which progressively weeds out poor black and brown folk, who have a much harder time securing the comparatively few highly desired places in higher education. These *de facto* failures of their own ideological ideals actually result in two salutary effects for white liberals: 1, more black and brown folk going through the prison system rather than the educational system means that white liberals face less competition in their niche of the labor market (i.e., positions that require higher education); 2, unable to enter the "skilled" sector of the labor market, black and brown folk disproportionately remain in the unskilled sector thus providing an overabundance of unskilled laborers. This overabundance of unskilled labor constitutes an economic boon for white liberals in that it leads to lower prices for the consumer goods and services that they rely upon. In fact, there is such a superabundance of unskilled labor that wages in these positions scarcely creep above minimum wage even with nearly 1% of the adult US population in prison at any given time. These supposed failures of liberal ideology actually work to inflate white liberals' living standards.

When redneck supported white supremacist policies and candidates win, white liberals share in the short-term benefits. In fact, white liberals may benefit from policies that run counter to their own ideological ideals even more than rednecks do. This is a difficult matter to calculate in exact terms. On the one hand, conservative policies mean jobs in the defense and prison industries, which are dominated by rednecks. On the other hand, however, because of their rural locales and their comparative lack of education, rednecks are less able than white liberals to procure the benefits of black and brown folk being kept out of the skilled sector of the labor market. While who benefits more (in the short-term) from white supremacist policies may be a matter that requires further investigation, that both rednecks and white liberals benefit from such policies is clear enough.

Contrary to the claims of Thomas Frank, for rednecks there is a clear tie between their own short-term economic interests and their chosen political ideology. However, when we add the variable of education, we see that white liberals benefit from *both* their own chosen political ideology *and* from the opposing political ideology of their redneck counterparts. The difference between white liberals and rednecks stems largely from the difference in their respective positions in relation to the social function of education. White liberals use their white privilege—derived from the historical and continuing use of white supremacy as an elite strategy to divide the working class amongst itself—in order to pursue education in the desperate attempt to flee the working class altogether. By contrast, generally speaking, rednecks rely upon securing the advantages of white supremacy while still remaining within the working class. Understanding the unique position of white liberals with respect to the social function of education is the key to understanding the complicated utility of white liberal political ideology.

Thinking of liberal ideology as a "triangulation" strategy—albeit on the part of a political base rather than a base's representatives, as the term is conventionally used—allows us to see the complex niche that white liberals have carved out for themselves in social and economic life. In other words, perhaps white liberals support policies and candidates that are somewhat to the left of their actual short-term interests because they know that these policies will be effectively curtailed by the policies and candidates supported by rednecks and the elite. Through such a process, not only do white liberals engineer a result that meets their interests—they also have the added ideological (and psychological) benefit of being able to claim that they are more sensitive to the humanitarian needs of the dark working class than are elites and rednecks. "Don't blame us!" white liberals can say to the dark working class with a clear conscience while at the same time reaping the benefits of those very exploitative policies.

If this sort of triangulation is an intentional strategy, it's positively ingenious; if its motivations are for the most part unconscious, nevertheless, it still works. Intentional or not, white liberals clearly do benefit in the short term from white supremacist policies—perhaps more than anyone else (with the noted exception of the rich). Of course, as ingenious as this strategy may be in the short term, in the long run it only consolidates the power of the rich thereby drawing ever closer the day when white liberals too will find themselves on the chopping block.

Perhaps white liberals are not as ingenious as this triangulation hypothesis would require them to be. However, the fact that they often benefit in the short-term from white supremacist policies goes a long way towards explaining why they are as forgiving as they are of the continual "failures" (if they can be so-called) of their elected officials to implement their stated ideology. Indeed, perhaps Bill Clinton's "triangulation"—seen in such white supremacist policies as welfare reform—really was indicative of an instinctive ability to read the true desires (as opposed to the stated ideologies) of his political base.

Appendices

Field Notes from *Blind Dog Café*: An Ethnography of a Coffee Shop for Young Urban White Liberals

Blind Dog Café is a coffee shop located in the Shaw neighborhood of Washington, DC. Centered around Howard University, Shaw has a distinguished history as a hotbed of black intellectual culture. As Wikipedia describes it:

> Shaw grew out of freed slave encampments in the rural outskirts of Washington City.... The neighborhood thrived in the late 19th and early 20th centuries as the pre-Harlem center of African-American intellectual and cultural life. Howard Theological Seminary received its first matriculates in 1866; by 1925, Professor Alain LeRoy Locke was advancing the idea of "The New Negro", and Langston Hughes was descending from LeDroit Park to hear the "sad songs" of 7th Street. The most famous Shaw native to emerge from this period—sometimes called the Harlem Renaissance—was Duke Ellington.

At present, alongside the extended, enthusiastic, and courteous greetings exchanged among longtime neighborhood folk, the daytime sounds most prevalent on Shaw's streets are the swinging of hammers and the buzzing of saws. In a wave of gentrification that was only briefly slowed by the mortgage crisis—real estate prices in much of DC are currently near their 2007 highs—Shaw's Victorian row houses are undergoing renovation at a frantic pace in order to appeal to the sensibilities of white liberal professionals flocking to the area primarily for its proximity to governmental and non-governmental ideological institutions (e.g., the White House is only two miles away). As opposed to their more conservative, generally older, and less culturally adventurous counterparts who live in Virginia, many of Shaw's new white liberal residents are in their 20s and 30s and appreciate (at least in theory) the idea of living in an area with such a rich history—provided that it looks and feels reasonably like the suburbs. The paramilitary policing of Shaw's black residents by DC Metro, to say nothing of the laundry list of additional federal law enforcement agencies with overlapping jurisdiction, has played a key role in facilitating the real estate turnover crucial to gentrification's acceleration. As Michelle Alexander notes in *The New Jim Crow*, "In Washington, D.C., our nation's capitol, it is estimated that three out of four young black men (and nearly all those in the poorest neighborhoods) can expect to serve time in prison."

Blind Dog Café is located in an old brick house on the corner of Florida Ave. and W St. No signage announces that the house in question is in fact a place of business. Besides its daytime manifestation as a café, the same calculatedly non-descript location also doubles as a nightclub. In the immediate proximity, besides the adjacent row houses and a couple of older warehouses, there stands two immense newly constructed condo towers of gleaming reflective glass and polished aluminum that could belong in any postmodern cityscape. In cumulative effect, the setting alone is enough to remind you of one of James Baldwin's particularly evocative essay titles: "Urban Renewal is Negro Removal." I was invited to a coffee meeting at *Blind Dog* by a well-meaning white liberal and below is my description of my first experience of the place upon arriving early.

I went to Blind Dog Café today and I don't think I can ever go there again. Unsure at first that the unmarked house was indeed the café that Google assured me was located at the designated address, I approached with a certain amount of trepidation. Nothing could be made out on the other side of the house's darkly shaded windows. Committed to the experiment of finding a locked door or god knows what on the other side, I turned the door handle. To my surprise, there was indeed a café! Coming out of the bright day and into the darkness, my eyes were met with a chalkboard menu primarily devoted to the adjectives belonging to a number of sandwiches and salads.

After buying my coffee, I proceeded to move to the adjacent sitting room. While making my way into the room, I was insulted for walking too slowly by a young white male with a short, squarish haircut who wore tight, knee-length jeans of neon green. "Think you can walk any slower?!" he shouted in my ear at a considerable volume from directly behind me. Startled, I nearly spilled the very hot cup of coffee that was the cause for my walking as slowly as I was. After the initial shock of this unexpected outburst, I was truly appalled at this young man's behavior. Who could be so crass as to attempt to publicly shame someone for their body not performing up to some kind of objective standard? Had these few seconds of life that he had lost really inconvenienced him so significantly as to warrant such a display of aggression? More perplexing still, a whole room of people witnessed this incident and said nothing about it to either me or him, as if there was nothing whatsoever remarkable about such behavior.

A few minutes went by and I sat quietly drinking my coffee, waiting for the person who'd suggested the location for our meeting. While waiting, I noticed that a woman sitting near me was grading a stack of papers and was in all likelihood a professor. I didn't want to disturb her but I thought I might try making some small talk, asking her what she taught, etc. As she stood up abruptly from her state of focused intensity—I remember that state, the games that you play with yourself to try to get through a stack of papers with reasonably consistent standards, how many can I do in 20 minutes, 40 minutes, an hour?—our eyes briefly crossed paths. Taking her coffee cup with her, it seemed she was on her way to get a refill. After taking an initial step towards the counter, however, she turned back and grabbed her laptop, looking accusingly at me as she did so, as if she was all too certain that I was determined to take advantage of the opportunity of her being a few steps away in a room full of people in order to deprive her of her brand new MacBook. I'm having a harder and harder time being around white people and the white people in DC are particularly obnoxious.

They are of such a marked difference in temperament from the black folks in this neighborhood. Even though from all outward appearances, I could simply be one more white liberal taking over the neighborhood, I have found time and again that the black folks here offer me greetings of deep cordiality for no reason besides our happening to occupy the same physical location at the same time, which upon reflection surely required any number of amazing accidents that neither of us will ever know. On the other hand, it is the group to which I am ostensibly a member, the group whose presence here is at the very least an indication of (and, in many respects, a cause of) the displacement of this neighborhood's pre-existing community, which makes me feel unwanted and unwelcome, an outcast, an outsider. For this young hip neoliberal cultural identity, you can be any gender, any color, any sexual orientation as long as you adopt the correct code, which is to say: YOU MUST DRESS AND ACT AND TALK LIKE US. DON'T TALK TO ME, I'M BUSY LOOKING AT FACEBOOK.

These people are deeply, deeply sick and the most tragic part is they have yet to realize it. To be in their presence pains me deeply. I want to help them but they are resolutely resistant to any sort of communication that they do not initiate. They live in a gated community of the mind. They are so deathly afraid of anything (and anyone) that they don't already know. Every interaction must be managed and fit into some sort of pre-existing conceptual slot ("work," "friends," "dating," "school," etc.). In many respects, this is the logical result of the micromanaged suburban childhoods which their parents programmed for them in order to ensure that they would have the best chance at getting into the right college. Then they go to college and succeed in some trivial sense but find that they have no idea who they are or what they want and not the slightest map as to how to figure those things out. Rather than confronting their own emptiness, instead they turn to resentment and snark (hence my slowness being an object of ridicule) and an aesthetics of ironic appropriation. The only value they believe in is the value that all values are equal and nothing should be valued too greatly.

There is of course, one thing that they cannot bear to talk about: money, where it comes from, where it goes, who has it, and who does not. Clinton's children. And as a consequence, they watch as every last bit of the welfare state is rolled back, they watch as the jobs that they studied for years in order to attain vanish, they watch as their loan payments skyrocket, they watch as they cannot afford to even think about things that their own parents took for granted like starting a family or buying a house. They watch because it is all they know how to do, all they've ever been taught to do. The truth is they don't believe in society any more than—no, quite possibly less than—Republicans.

They may say they want to build community, but they have no idea how to do it because they have no models for how to have real human relationships outside of a predetermined context. Relationships exist first and foremost for no purpose other than human sociality. Encounter one another as singular, real, distinct, unique bodies, minds, histories, identities, needs, and abilities and see what unfolds from there.

Appendix B
White Liberals at the End of Mass Media

The power elite, especially the liberal elite, has always been willing to sacrifice integrity and truth for power, personal advancement, foundation grants, awards, tenured professorships, columns, book contracts, television appearances, generous lecture fees and social status. They know what they need to say. They know which ideology they have to serve. They know what lies must be told—the biggest being that they take moral stances on issues that aren't safe and anodyne. They have been at this game a long time. And they will, should their careers require it, happily sell us out again.

- *Chris Hedges*, "Treason of the Intellectuals[17]

As a paradigmatic institution of white liberal collaborationism, the mainstream media is an example as obvious as it is instructive. In order to illustrate the essential role of white liberal institutions in supporting the very policies that are hypothetically contrary to the liberal world view, let's take a brief stroll through a bit of recent history, which may indeed be the most distant of all. I ask you: would the Iraq War have been possible if it was not sold to the public by the New York Times and many other mainstream outlets that are indeed run largely by white liberals? Would the country really have been convinced—or, at any rate, made less insistent

[17]

http://www.truthdig.com/report/print/the_treason_of_the_intellectuals_20130331/

concerning their suspicion of the employees of an unelected president—by Fox News and talk radio alone? Upon reflection, almost certainly not.

To take The New York Times and The LA Times as particular examples, it is all too apparent that the decision of the papers to support the War was not simply a natural outgrowth of the white liberal groupthink and deference to authority that is generally endemic to such institutions. While most journalists accepted their marching orders without question from the government sources who all-too transparently sought the media's influence in building popular support for the War, there were a few who did not and their cases are particularly instructive. When journalists as entrenched in the white liberal media establishment as Robert Scheer and Chris Hedges dared to question the wisdom of the War and the veracity of the intelligence upon which the case for war was made, they soon found themselves unceremoniously dismissed by their longtime employers. That firing such respected senior journalists for the sin of ideological dissent would have a chilling effect upon the willingness of younger journalists employed at such institutions to question government authorities is so obvious a consequence that it must be seen as intended. In many respects, that chilling effect has persisted in the reporting of such institutions to the present day.

Hedges' recent assessment of the truly remarkable degree of liberal collaborationism in paving the way for the Iraq War is deeply instructive:

The rewriting of history by the power elite was painfully evident as the nation marked the 10th anniversary of the start of the Iraq War. Some claimed they had opposed the war when they had not. Others among "Bush's useful idiots" argued that they had merely acted in good faith on the information available; if they had known then what they know now, they assured us, they would have acted differently. This, of course, is false. The war boosters, especially the "liberal hawks"—who included Hillary Clinton, Chuck Schumer, Al Franken and John Kerry, along with academics, writers and journalists such as Bill Keller, Michael Ignatieff, Nicholas Kristof, David Remnick,Fareed Zakaria, Michael Walzer, Paul Berman, Thomas Friedman, George Packer,Anne-Marie Slaughter, Kanan Makiya and the late Christopher Hitchens—did what they always have done: engage in acts of self-preservation. To oppose the war would have been a career killer. And they knew it.

Ten years later, where is the kind of *mea culpa* writ large from liberal war boosters that even the most minimal standard of sincerity would seem to require given the fact that it is now an undisputed fact that the WMD intelligence was complete and total horseshit? Where is the robustly adversarial stance toward government authority that is the only possible protection from that authority's worst excesses and abuses? What could be a more serious injury to the well-being of a democratic society than manipulating the public into war? For that matter, what could be a greater crime against humanity than an unnecessary war?

In a society that took such offenses seriously, The NY Times' Judith Miller and the editors who enabled her (Bill Keller in particular) would share a cell with Dick Cheney. For that matter, Tony Blair and the Democratic Senators named by Hedges above (many of whom are still in office and doing their best to collaborate with Republicans in foisting economic austerity upon American taxpayers; after all, such a strategy proved so effective in extricating Europe from the financial crisis created by the reckless criminality of the world's major banks) would be down the hall in the same prison. It would be poetic justice for white political and media criminals from across the political spectrum to see the inside of a penal institution. After all, under their not so benign neglect (and, in some cases, outright collusion) the criminal justice system's dehumanization of black and brown men for minor drug offenses (despite the criminological fact that whites are just as likely to commit such offenses) allowed the construction and operation of prisons to become a conspicuously prominent feature of the economy in many regions of the country.

Far from being locked up for their crimes against democracy, many of the white liberals of the mainstream media continue their work today, unabated in their abdication of the public trust and as deferential to authority and ideological consensus as ever. If it seems as if the white liberal media establishment is completely unaware of the horrific consequences of their past servility, it is because they probably are. Such a willful ignorance is almost certainly essential if they are to continue to please the corporate overlords who hold their jobs on a string.

It is telling indeed that at present, the closest thing to ideologically dissonant voices among the ranks of the mainstream media's plethora of white liberal commentators are Paul Krugman and Joseph Stiglitz, both of whom are allowed a place to speak only due to their intellectual contributions to the present edifice of capitalist economics. It seems that no one in the white liberal media establishment is willing or able to go as far in their critique of the corporate oligarchy that plunders the country's health and well-being as the Directors of the Federal Reserve's Dallas and St. Louis branches, both of whom have declaimed unequivocally that the major banks must be broken up before the economy can recover in any meaningful sense.[18] Even Ben Bernanke has adopted this view, and yet such an opinion still remains far, far too radical for the media's white liberals.

It is a sad, sad day when (even if only out of political opportunism) certain Republican senators are more willing than mainstream journalists to ask the hard questions concerning the government's role in the execution of war. As the Executive claims the unprecedented authority to oversee an assassination

---

[18] The director of the Dallas Fed, Richard W. Fisher, has a quite detailed proposal regarding how to go about ending the "too big too fail" problem with respect to large banks.
http://www.dallasfed.org/news/speeches/fisher/2013/fs130116.cfm

program, the press offers no significant objections. Perhaps even more disturbingly, the press is all but entirely silent concerning the Executive's vicious and vengeful campaign to use the most exotic of legal pretexts to prosecute whistleblowers (such as Thomas Drake, John Kiriakou, and Chelsea Manning) who dared to expose government lies to the public. In the face of such undeniable abuses of power in the name of national security, the white liberals in the media are unable to respond with even a modicum of the courage shown by the whistleblowers themselves, who put not only their careers but their lives on the line for the sake of bringing to light the uncomfortable truths concerning government deeds.

Bill Keller's remarks in the wake of Manning's claim that The Times ignored her attempts to get into contact with them are particularly instructive here:

> If Manning had connected with The Times, we would have found ourselves in a relationship with a nervous, troubled, angry young Army private who was offering not so much documentation of a particular government outrage as a chance to fish in a sea of secrets. Having never met Manning (he was in custody by the time we got the WikiLeaks documents), I can only guess what that relationship would have been like. Complicated. Probably tense.[...] Once he was arrested, we'd surely have editorialized against the brutality of his solitary confinement — as The Times has already done — and perhaps protested the disturbing overkill of the "aiding the enemy" charge.[...] Beyond that, we'd have made sure Manning knew upfront that he was

on his own, as we did with the last leaker of this magnitude, Daniel Ellsberg of Pentagon Papers fame.

What a resounding statement of support for an act of such remarkable courage and incalculable risk, an act that's consequences have incontestably changed the face of the world for the better, an act that has done more to foster peace than nearly any other of recent memory! The most essential social function of the press in a democracy—providing the public with the truth as to what their government is actually doing in their name—depends almost entirely upon inside sources being willing to disclose information at great potential harm. We can be assured that the less supported and defended whistleblowers are in their disclosures, the less championed their rights and cause, the greater will be the harm that comes to them. In turn, the less likely it will be that other whistleblowers will come forward in the future and the less the public will know about government corruption, deception, fraud, and abuse.

As the remarks of Hedges suggest, it is for a simple and obvious reason that the war-enabling white liberals of the media are as hesitant to support Manning as they are. What reporter at a major paper would willingly compromise his access to the next pre-manufactured fluff story to come out of the White House? Such a lack of access might very well mean the end of a career. The reality is: we live in a time and a place where journalists who ask serious questions lose their jobs. The true tragedy is that there aren't more of them who are willing to face such consequences. That level of commitment to the truth and nothing less is what it will take to shatter the bipartisan political consensus that finds it perfectly acceptable to kill the poor (both abroad and at home) as long as the rich can make money while doing it.

Acts of courage and risk like Manning's are what it will take to breathe life back into the farce of democracy. The bureaucrats who execute our wars have a natural incentive to do everything in their power to discourage such acts of heroism from occurring in the future. In the interest of their own self-preservation and in direct contradiction to the public interest, government bureaucrats can be counted on to see to it that whistleblowers are punished with the greatest possible severity. The only possible check upon our representatives' ability to undermine the very core of the political system in which they serve is the public's own readiness to censure any and all public officials who treat the disclosure of state crimes as a sin greater than the crimes themselves. What more essential and relevant, as opposed to immediately profitable, function could there be for the press than to aid the public in this regard?

The short-term cost savings found in access-driven fluff journalism come at the direct expense of the press' own social relevance. It might be argued that the complacency of journalism is inevitable in an era in which the advertising-driven model of media funding is increasingly in doubt. Given the ongoing difficulty of papers to pay for primary reporting, perhaps the economic basis simply isn't there to support dissident voices. Yes, we certainly do need to promote and create more non-profit sources for funding real reporting and investigative journalism in particular. However, the most immediate question that should be asked is: if we took great pains to isolate the corporate and governmental shills in the media, to the point that the media's most enduring institutions were completely devoid of any and all legitimacy, would such a loss really be so detrimental? What would we have to lose besides the next great war? In the new media economy, it is the consciously oppositional reporters such as Jeremy Scahill, Glenn Greenwald, and Matt Taibbi who have not only found an audience but who continue to thrive. It still seems to be the case that, in one manner or another, the public is willing to pay for reporting if and when they are given something worth paying for.

White liberals! For once in your life grow a fucking backbone! The world may need you but the world won't *wait* for you. Ask some tough questions for once in your life! Follow up! Demand the truth! Burn all your bridges and contacts who expect you to look the other way! Work with your white liberal lawyer friends and sue the bastards! Tell the public who is responsible and tell them to get angry!

I recognize this advice is vague. I understand that you're still so unaware of the narrowness of your ideological constraints that naturally it makes it difficult for you to see the limits of those constraints.

If you want to prove that I'm wrong about you, that you're not really a creature whose existence depends essentially upon timidity and deference to authority, then you should have no problem committing yourself to a *bona fides* test.

Recall firstly that the crimes of war in Afghanistan and Iraq were largely an outgrowth of the social psychological climate of security hysteria that followed in the wake of 9/11 and the Anthrax Attacks (and the license to conduct these war crimes in turn enabled the defense industry's looting of the US Treasury to the tune of trillions of dollars). White liberals, I challenge you to seriously investigate the following questions just as you would any other empirical questions that you regard as hypothetically plausible but needing subsequent confirmation:

First of all, are you really so sure that the Anthrax Attacks were the product of the lone nut, Bruce Ivins, as the FBI claims?[19] Who was it that performed a series of very lucrative informed options trades on the stocks of major airlines in the days leading up to 9/11?[20]

---

[19] See: Glenn Greenwald, "Serious Doubt Cast on FBI Case against Bruce Ivins," http://www.salon.com/2011/02/16/ivans/ Also, Prof. Graeme MacQueen's debunking of the lone nut hypothesis concerning the Anthrax Attacks in a talk he gave at Harvard University in May 2010: http://www.youtube.com/watch?v=j0Bu-0-eKJI

[20] In their rigorous econometric study "Detecting Informed Trading Activities in the Options Market," Chesney, Crameri, and Mancini analyze the stocks of 31 different companies over a period of 14 years in the effort to detect informed options trades. Selecting for only significantly lucrative options trades of unusually high volume, only 37 trades over this 14 year period

Why wasn't Abdussattar Shaikh, an FBI informant with whom two of the alleged hijackers (Hazmi and Mihdhar) lived for at least four months, ever interviewed by the 9/11 Commission?[21] What is the explanation for the documented presence of nanothermitic material in the World Trade Center dust?[22] Or for the fact that frame analysis of the video evidence of the collapse of the South Tower shows objects of debris accelerating downward *faster* than the speed of gravity?[23] How was it common

---

were identified as informed trades through this particularly restrictive methodology. Amazingly, 13 of these abnormally lucrative trades took place two weeks or less prior to 9/11 allowing these traders to benefit directly from the drop in stock prices for the companies in question following 9/11. The question is simple: Who made these 13 trades? The article of Chesney, et al is available here:
http://www.bf.uzh.ch/publikationen/pdf/4007.pdf
For an excellent lay summary of the complex statistical work of Chesney, et al see Paul Zarembka's article "Evidence of Insider Trading before September 11th Re-examined":
http://ithp.org/articles/septemberinsidertrading.html
[21] That Mihdhar and Hazmi both lived with Shaikh is openly acknowledged by the FBI themselves. From the FBI's post-9/11 internal review: "In late January 2000, Mihdhar and Hazmi both traveled to Los Angeles and then moved to San Diego, where they associated with a former subject of an FBI investigation and also lived with a long-time FBI asset." What did Shaikh know about Hazmi and Mihdhar's plans and when did he know it? Did he report it to the FBI? If not, why not?
http://www.justice.gov/oig/special/0506/chapter5.htm
[22] Dr. Niels Harrit provided an excellent summary of much of the research concerning the presence of explosive nanothermitic material in samples of WTC dust at the Toronto Hearings of 2011: http://www.youtube.com/watch?v=uNPeMvsSbl4

knowledge that WTC Building 7 would collapse several hours before the fact, as reported by a number of mainstream media outlets, when never before in history had a steel-framed building ever collapsed due to fire?[24]

All I ask is for your willingness to suspend certainty in the process of investigating the evidence provided. After investigating these questions, perhaps your initial suspicions will be confirmed. But then perhaps they won't. Honestly what result are you more scared of? Anyone more afraid of uncomfortable truths than comfortable lies will find themselves bound to live a life wholly determined by the latter.

---

[23] The physicist David Chandler provides documentation and measurement of the object moving faster than the speed of gravity during the collapse of the South Tower here: http://www.youtube.com/watch?v=xvw0_i1rGns&list=UUxvGFyC UkbMk4pB0C-AUJwQ&index=2
Chandler's physical analysis of the collapse of WTC Building 7 at the Toronto Hearings is also well worth watching: http://www.youtube.com/watch?v=UErOy9lwfhc
[24] For an exhaustive compendium of the numerous media reports that demonstrate what can only be regarded as a remarkable level of foreknowledge concerning an event that had no comparable historical precedent (the collapse of a steel-framed building due to fire), see Graeme MacQueen's presentation from April of 2011 available here: http://www.youtube.com/watch?v=McF4flr2dYs

Appendix C
The Death of a White Liberal

In our culture... strength is not enough. One must be born without blemish, and be strong and brilliant on top of that. Yang is critical of Aaron's inability to endure pointless things thrust on him by corrupt power structures. I share this quality with Aaron, so I am left asking myself, why am I alive? I believe it is for two reasons: I was born a woman, and I was born poor. To be either in America teaches you something quickly that Aaron never learned. It teaches you that you are prey. I have the instincts of a prey animal: avoid detection, flee from violent people, hide, wait, use all available resources for my advantage. Aaron and I were both fragile, but he believed that we still lived in a society that valued something other than might and force. I have no such illusions.

- *Quinn Norton*[25]

White liberals: Aaron Swartz died for *your* sins. As badly as you treat those who disagree with you in principle or in fact, you are perhaps even more vicious to those who act upon the deepest liberal convictions to the extent that those convictions require if they are to mean anything at all. You insist that these convictions, the very convictions that define your own

---

[25] Norton's reflections on the social significance of Aaron Swartz' death are deeply moving and worth reading in their entirety. http://www.quinnnorton.com/said/?p=678
Norton is referring to Wesley Yang's New York Magazine article, "The Life and Afterlife of Aaron Swartz," http://nymag.com/news/features/aaron-swartz-2013-2/

ideological position, must remain in the non-realized realm of pure ideals, guiding action only by the most compromised and measured of approximations. You like your ideals kept clean from the messy consequences that are almost certain to follow from their direct engenderment in reality. I ask you white liberals: at the end of the day, what are all your ideals worth? How can you expect anyone else to take these ideals seriously when you yourself hesitate to put them into practice?

When I say Aaron Swartz died for the sins of white liberals, let me be specific about whom I'm accusing and the grounds upon which I'm making such an accusation. Obviously, first and foremost, I'm talking about the bloodthirsty liberals in the Department of Justice—lapdogs of the powerful that they are—who routinely and deliberately overlook the most venial of crimes (e.g., the nearly billion dollars worth of drug laundering by HSBC, the systematic fabrication of mortgage documents in foreclosure claims, the majestic violation of the public trust found in the Bush Administration's systematic distortion and fabrication of intelligence leading to the Iraq War; we could go on) in order to throw the full investigative and accusatory weight of the federal government behind the prosecution of the smallest of infractions, be they real or perceived. Only in exceptionally rare instances need the government ever prove its cases on their own merits, for when your authority to make threats is nearly unlimited, so is your ability to compel confessions. This was precisely the strategy adopted by the government in Aaron's case, not, I don't think, out of any particular malice above and beyond that which constitutes the general *modus operandi* of the *criminal* justice system in this country.

If there is anything remarkable about the judicial overreach seen in Aaron's case it's that for once the government was actually bothering to take on someone with not inconsiderable resources behind him (as compared to, e.g., the vast preponderance of poor, black, and brown folk who are at this moment doing time for drug offenses). Aaron's prosecution need be seen as part of a larger strategy of more aggressive digital copyright enforcement on the part of the Obama administration. One might think that liberals would take a more lax position toward copyright enforcement than their conservative counterparts given the fact that one of, if not *the*, most fundamental values of liberalism is the conviction that the *free* dissemination of information should be assumed as socially beneficial until and unless it is proven otherwise. But then, with respect to the Obama Administration's fascist interpretation of liberalism, one would be wrong.[26] As Chris Meadows writes:

---

[26] I do not use the word fascist lightly. The curtailing of individual rights (with respect to, e.g., due process, freedom of speech, unionization, basic housing and subsistence, etc.) in order to facilitate the collusion of government and industry power is indeed an apt description of many Obama Administration policies (e.g., the extrajudicial assassination program run out of the Oval Office, the federally coordinated crackdown on the Occupy movement, the state-enforced payments to private

Under the Obama Administration, the government has promoted "[number of] strikes" laws or programs in which ISPs would cut off their users after a certain number of copyright violations. It has seized hundreds of allegedly-infringing websites without due process. It has also crusaded with trade negotiations to try to get other countries to tighten up their copyright restrictions after the American model. The whole thing is more than a little ironic given how many copyright reform crusaders come from the left—indeed, Larry Lessig himself...[27]

---

insurance companies compelled by the "individual mandate" component of Obamacare, the use of the Espionage Act with unprecedented frequency to prosecute whistleblowers who expose government crimes, providing an unlimited amount of zero-interest loans—i.e., free money—to the biggest banks, refusing to make any serious inquiry into the vast and systematic operational fraud that resulted in hundreds of thousands of unlawful evictions throughout the country; we could go on).

[27] http://www.the-digital-reader.com/2012/09/05/for-democrats-internet-freedom-means-vigorous-copyright-enforcement/#.UWW9IJNg-gk

See also: Ben Sheffner, "Entertainment Unions, Trade Associations Thank Obama for Support of Copyright Enforcement, ACTA"
http://copyrightsandcampaigns.blogspot.com/2010/03/entertainment-unions-trade-associations.html

And: Jason Mick, "Obama Conscripts ISPs as 'Copyright Cops', Unveils ' Six Strikes' Plan"
http://www.dailytech.com/Obama+Conscripts+ISPs+as+Copyright+Cops+Unveils+Six+Strikes+Plan/article22107.htm

For an excellent guide on relatively simple ways to avoid triggering the Copyright Alert System maintained by ISPs while

Indeed, I doubt very much that Aaron's case would have been prosecuted, much less to the extent that it was, under the Bush Administration for the simple reason that the offended parties—JSTOR and MIT of course, but also and perhaps more importantly, copyright holders more generally, that is to say, first and foremost, Hollywood—were all white liberal institutions. Copyright holders are not just any white liberals. They are what we might call, the *real* white liberals in that they are the small subset of rich white liberals who in many cases gave lots of money to put Obama and many other (primarily Democratic) politicians in office. Thank goodness our system is as simple as it is: You pays your money, you gets your laws. Indeed, it is only thanks to the dogged efforts of a vast array of moderately compensated white liberals that we are hesitant to remark upon just how simple our system actually is or to call that simplicity by its most obvious name: corruption.

With good reason, we can claim that even though they may not have in any way directly interceded in Aaron's case, any of the various white liberal institutions, who petitioned (and, more importantly, *paid*) the Obama Administration for more aggressive copyright enforcement (the RIAA and the MPAA in particular) provided a compelling motivation for Aaron's prosecution. Indeed, given his invaluable role

---

sharing files, see this article by Kevin Collier from Feb. 25, 2013: http://www.dailydot.com/news/copyright-alerts-how-to-download-upload-hide/

in the Stop SOPA campaign that showed a considerable influence in slowing the progress of corporate-governmental digital tyranny, Aaron was a particularly sensible target for the Justice Department to take aim at as a means of pleasing their corporate and governmental masters. Thus, the Hollywood liberals who provided the cash incentives for Aaron's prosecution share a good deal of the responsibility for his death alongside the Justice Department liberals who heeded the orders of the liberal politicians accepting those cash incentives.

Aaron's case is a paradigmatic one for examining the vengeance that white liberals can unleash upon those closest to their ideals who they nevertheless perceive as compromising their immediate political and economic interests. Indeed, as much as his actions conformed to the fundamental ideals of liberalism itself, Aaron nevertheless committed what for white liberals must be considered the most grave— if not the only unpardonable—sin: he acted upon his beliefs directly without compromising and without deference to legislative, judicial, and/or institutional policy and authority. On this point, Aaron's own "Guerrilla Open Access Manifesto" is worth quoting at length:

> The world's entire scientific and cultural heritage, published over centuries in books and journals, is increasingly being digitized and locked up by a handful of private corporations. Want to read the papers featuring the most famous results

of the sciences? You'll need to send enormous amounts to publishers like Reed Elsevier.

That is too high a price to pay. Forcing academics to pay money to read the work of their colleagues? Scanning entire libraries but only allowing the folks at Google to read them? Providing scientific articles to those at elite universities in the First World, but not to children in the Global South? It's outrageous and unacceptable.[...]

Those with access to these resources — students, librarians, scientists — you have been given a privilege. You get to feed at this banquet of knowledge while the rest of the world is locked out. But you need not —indeed, morally, you cannot — keep this privilege for yourselves. You have a duty to share it with the world. And you have: trading passwords with colleagues, filling download requests for friends. [...]But all of this action goes on in the dark, hidden underground. It's called stealing or piracy, as if sharing a wealth of knowledge were the moral equivalent of plundering a ship and murdering its crew. But sharing isn't immoral — it's a moral imperative.[...] Large corporations, of course, are blinded by greed. The laws under which they operate require it — their shareholders would revolt at anything less. And the politicians they have bought off back them, passing laws giving them the exclusive power to decide who can make copies.

There is no justice in following unjust laws. It's time to come into the light and, in the grand tradition of civil disobedience, declare our opposition to this private theft of public culture.[28]

There is a contradiction at the heart of the liberal tradition between belief and action and Aaron's case illustrates exactly this contradiction. On the one hand, liberals hold that the expression of belief should take place in a fashion that is as absolute, free, and unrestrained as possible. On the other hand, when it comes to acting upon beliefs, they insist that we must be as moderate, cautious, careful, judicious, temperate, and restrained as possible. It is the temperance of liberal action that justifies the ideal of supposedly absolute freedom of debate. Theoretically speaking, the contradiction is this: until and unless beliefs are put into action, they mean nothing whatsoever and wherever and whenever we refuse to put our deepest beliefs into action directly, we thereby lose any and all legitimate claim to those beliefs. Practically speaking, the contradiction is this: it is only through direct action that the means to engage in infinite dialogue and debate ever exist.

Some *one* has to publish the unpublishable. Some *one* has to say the unsayable. Unless some *one* takes it upon themselves to disseminate knowledge by the most widely accessible, most freely available, most readily sharable means that knowledge ceases to be. Nay, any "knowledge" that lacks its widest conceivable audience of adherents, critics, admirers, skeptics,

---

[28]

http://ia600808.us.archive.org/17/items/GuerillaOpenAccessManif esto/Goamjuly2008.pdf experts, and lay persons alike wherever these persons may happen to be located on the globe and regardless of their ability to pay never amounts to knowledge in any meaningful sense of the word in the first place. There is nothing particularly novel or radical about such a view. Among other places, it can be found implied in that most canonically liberal text, Mill's *On Liberty*:

> The whole strength and value, then, of human judgment, depending on the one property, that it can be set right when it is wrong, reliance can be placed on it only when the means of setting it right are kept constantly at hand. In the case of any person whose judgment is really deserving of confidence, how has it become so?[...] Because he has felt, that the only way in which a human being can make some approach to knowing the whole of a subject, is by hearing what can be said about it by persons of every variety of opinion, and studying all modes in which it can be looked at by every character of mind.[29]

The standard of knowledge that Mill proposes here (i.e., that any given idea be looked at by "*every* variety of opinion" and "*every* character of mind") is an absolute one. The only limitations it implies are practical (e.g., time constraints) and in effect largely technological. The act of collective striving that is the *process* of knowledge itself presupposes that, while this absolute standard may never be met in practice,

---

[29] http://www.gutenberg.org/files/34901/34901-h/34901-h.htm

nor must it ever be transgressed in fact. Any means of dissemination that is anything less than the most accessible of those available at a given place and time constitutes a *de facto* transgression to the intent inherent to the existence of knowledge as a social (f)act.

Thus, not only can and should Aaron's actions be read as entirely consistent with the most uncontroversial and widely accepted doctrines of liberalism; according to the very standard articulated in that tradition's most rigorous and thoughtful formulations, the ideals of liberalism would themselves cease to mean anything whatsoever without the constant presence of transgressive unsanctioned unapproved unpermitted acts of conscience like Aaron's. There can be no such thing as liberalism, no such thing as freedom of speech, no such thing as knowledge, until and unless some *one* acts in the interest of the silenced majority. Anyone anywhere who is kept without the means to express themselves by private interests when those means would otherwise be available constitutes a silenced majority. I use the phrase "silenced majority" because we must assume *until proven otherwise* that any opinion or minority that is deemed so dangerous by the powers that be that it is routinely silenced, ignored, and/or criminalized must have at least some potentially influential aspect, however minimal.

Majorities can only ever be *un*silenced when and insofar as they have at their disposal any and all means that could possibly prove useful in aiding them to exert their greatest potential influence. Obviously, the unfettered access to the most influential sources of knowledge plays an extremely significant role in the process of *un*silencing the majority. There where there is exclusion, such as with respect to the paywalls that guard supposedly "scientific" journals, knowledge withers and becomes something less than itself. We cannot know in advance the detrimental effects *to the majority* of silencing what may seem the most tangential or minoritarian of bodies. It is not enough simply to do nothing as doing nothing is equivalent to letting the minority of already established interests decide what gets to be said and who gets to say it. *Un*silencing the majority always takes direct action so as to ensure that the tools of influence are available as widely as possible, so that any and all minorities can present their case in the best possible terms and so that, finally, and only in the degree to which the process itself is absolute, a true majority will emerge.

In order to open up such a space of free dissemination, some *one* must take a risk by acting *against* the prevailing protocols found in social decorum, privately arranged contracts, narrowly decided legal precedents, and narrowly written legislation. The very separation of free, unfettered, open, unrestrained, unlimited thought from cautious, judicious, diffident action upon which liberalism rests itself requires that some *one* act dangerously, even recklessly, so as to maintain the freedom of thought in practice. Without the actual realm of thought fulfilling the ideals of openness and accessibility to the greatest extent technologically possible at a given time and place, the liberal promise not to act precipitously—to consider the matter at hand from all possible views, to be as resolutely unprejudiced regarding the available options as one is able—is completely and utterly meaningless.

This is why I say that Aaron died for your sins, white liberals. Until and unless you act in order to fulfill your ideals *in the one fashion that your ideals themselves unequivocally demand,* until and unless you throw the whole weight of your being behind your convictions to the point that you willingly incur any and all civil penalties and sanctions that your actions provoke *whatever their nature,* until and unless that day of action comes then *you,* my white liberal friend, are the most effective agent of the destruction of your own ideals.

Afterword

While I would no longer call myself a white liberal, perhaps as a consequence of the way I was raised— and certainly as a consequence of the diverse social forces that forged me—I can't help but feel a deep and enduring commitment to the Unitarian-inflected expression of universal human dignity. In the final analysis, as a consequence of these socially-formed values perhaps, but not, I hope, without reason, I want to affirm that *no one* benefits from white supremacy. This is not nearly the same thing as the popular Christian fiction that those who do evil will be punished in the by and by, a claim for which I see no evidence either in this life or the next one. Rather, it is the assertion—irrelevant until and unless it is put into the most steadfast and uncompromising practice— that a more just society, a more equitable society, a more open society is a more dynamic society, a more interesting society, and a more fulfilling society for all parties concerned.

ABOUT THE AUTHOR

Marc Lombardo is an independent thinker, essayist, philosopher, poet, blogger, and activist. After receiving his doctorate from European Graduate School, where he studied with many of contemporary Continental philosophy's most recognized figures, Marc has gone on to a life of varied intellectual struggle. Marc was deeply transformed by his participation with the Occupy movement from which he has taken the enduring conviction that a better world is not only possible but practically workable as well. His scholarly articles have appeared in *Contemporary Pragmatism* and *Journal of Speculative Philosophy*. With any luck, Marc's landmark philosophical treatise, *Critique of Sovereignty*, will meet the public soon. He occasionally updates the blog *Once, Again* (11again.wordpress.com) and tweets as @aliveoccupation.

www.ingramcontent.com/pod-product-compliance
Lightning Source LLC
Chambersburg PA
CBHW022107280326
41933CB00007B/295